KRAFTS FOR KIDS

Origami

KRAFTS FOR KIDS

Origami

Gillian Johnson-Flint

CHARTWELL
BOOKS, INC.

A QUINTET BOOK

Published by Chartwell Books, Inc.
A Division of Book Sales, Inc.
114 Northfield Avenue
Edison, New Jersey 08837

This edition produced for sale in the U.S.A.,
its territories and dependencies only.

ISBN 0-7858-0620-2

This book was designed and produced by
Quintet Publishing Limited
6 Blundell Street
London N7 9BH

Creative Director: Richard Dewing
Designer: Ian Hunt
Senior Editor: Anna Briffa
Editor: Amanda Horton
Photographer: Colin Bowling
Hand Model: Emma Penfold

Typeset in Great Britain by
Central Southern Typesetters, Eastbourne
Manufactured in Singapore by
Bright Arts Pte Ltd
Printed in China by
Leefung-Asco Printers Ltd

ACKNOWLEDGMENTS

Special thanks to:

Maureen and Christine Abbott for
typing the manuscript

Scott and Claire Harrington,
Arron Charles, Tom Lolobo and
Azaria Gairy-Newbolt,
Spencer and Victoria Dewing

Family and friends for
encouragement and support

A & J Lampshade Frames for
making the frames

Paperchase, London,
for providing art materials

PUBLISHER'S NOTE
Children should take great care when completing
these projects. Certain tools and techniques, such as
craft knives and using the oven, can be dangerous
and extreme care must be exercised at all times.
Adults should always supervise while children work
on the projects.
As far as methods and techniques mentioned in this
book are concerned, all statements, information and
advice given here are believed to be true and
accurate. However, the author, copyright holder, and
the publisher cannot accept legal liability for errors
or omissions.

Contents

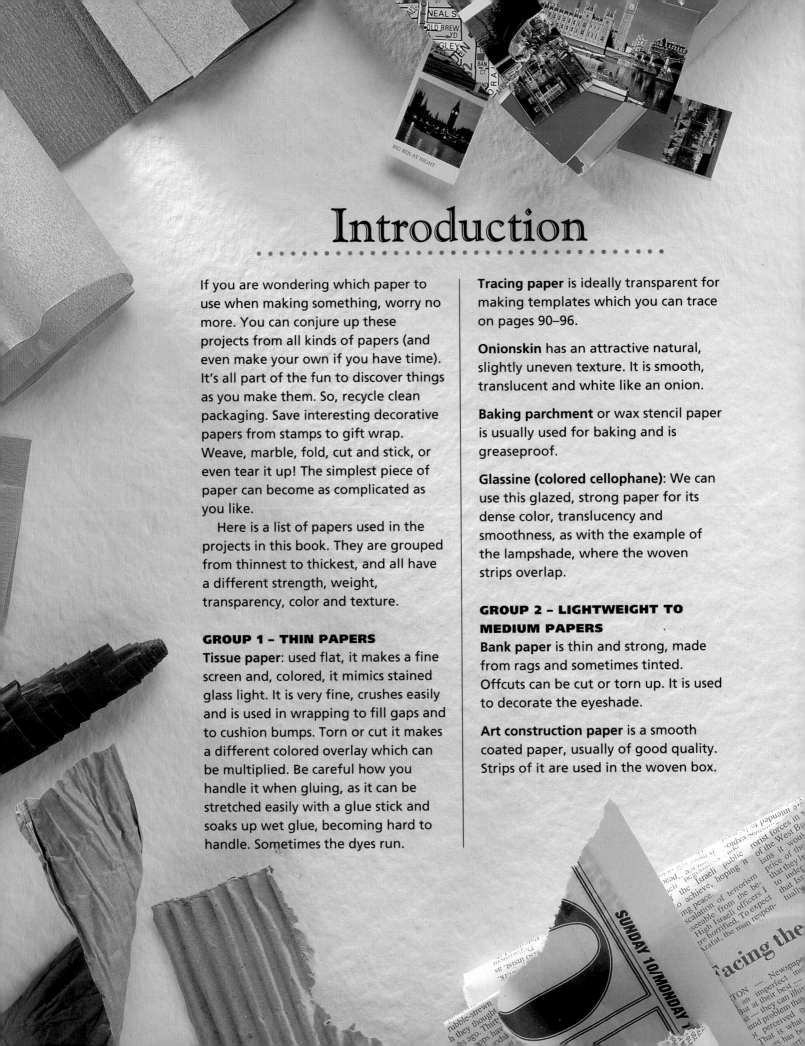

Introduction

If you are wondering which paper to use when making something, worry no more. You can conjure up these projects from all kinds of papers (and even make your own if you have time). It's all part of the fun to discover things as you make them. So, recycle clean packaging. Save interesting decorative papers from stamps to gift wrap. Weave, marble, fold, cut and stick, or even tear it up! The simplest piece of paper can become as complicated as you like.

Here is a list of papers used in the projects in this book. They are grouped from thinnest to thickest, and all have a different strength, weight, transparency, color and texture.

GROUP 1 – THIN PAPERS

Tissue paper: used flat, it makes a fine screen and, colored, it mimics stained glass light. It is very fine, crushes easily and is used in wrapping to fill gaps and to cushion bumps. Torn or cut it makes a different colored overlay which can be multiplied. Be careful how you handle it when gluing, as it can be stretched easily with a glue stick and soaks up wet glue, becoming hard to handle. Sometimes the dyes run.

Tracing paper is ideally transparent for making templates which you can trace on pages 90–96.

Onionskin has an attractive natural, slightly uneven texture. It is smooth, translucent and white like an onion.

Baking parchment or wax stencil paper is usually used for baking and is greaseproof.

Glassine (colored cellophane): We can use this glazed, strong paper for its dense color, translucency and smoothness, as with the example of the lampshade, where the woven strips overlap.

GROUP 2 – LIGHTWEIGHT TO MEDIUM PAPERS

Bank paper is thin and strong, made from rags and sometimes tinted. Offcuts can be cut or torn up. It is used to decorate the eyeshade.

Art construction paper is a smooth coated paper, usually of good quality. Strips of it are used in the woven box.

Crepe paper is crinkled and lightweight. It stretches so that one can mold it between the thumbs into rounded shapes, making more realistic petals as in the sunflower.

Color magazines, catalogs or tourist brochures are handy to collect for découpage or torn picture work on cards.

Brown wrapping paper makes a good wrapper or envelope, and is combined with corrugated cardboard in the letter holder.

Poster paper is available in many strong colors on single sides only. It is ideal for origami.

Pastel or tinted paper has a slightly rough texture. It makes an ideal background for the bookmark.

Newsprint is cheaply made from wood pulp and makes good papier-mâché, as it is easy to tear up and soaks up paste readily.

Activity or craft paper is sold in a choice of thicknesses and has dense colors. It is useful for folded cards, pop-ups and torn up decorations over papier mâché, as in the pen tray.

Construction paper is a cheaper, uncoated paper of medium or heavy weight and is made in various shades. It is useful for crayon or colored pencil work as with the pop-up pig cards.

Burmese lizard paper or lizard wyndstone paper has a printed, textured surface like this animal's skin.

Cover paper is nearly as thick as some cards. Specially made for bookbinding, it is usually found in darker shades and is used in the marbled stationery folder.

GROUP 3 – CARDS AND BOARDS

Card may be plain, or textured like hammer–embossed card. The thin, bendable card used in the outside lantern provides good support for colored tissue in windows. Thicker card, printed black on one side (reused packaging), is used in making the woven box.

Board is made up in what is called "sheets" in thickness. There is a heavy–sheet board but 6–sheet board is strong enough for the marbled stationery folder.

Foamboard is thick but light, filled with polystyrene foam and is used for the frame holding the mobiles.

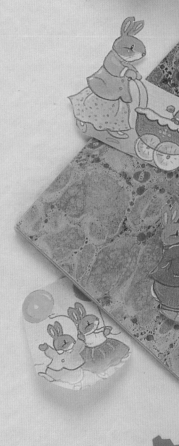

TOOLS

I worked out, in order of priority, how often I have used the tools needed on projects for this book. To highlight safety some of the photographs are bordered with red warning triangles and the instructions are written in bold underlined text.

HB pencil well–sharpened comes top of the list. It is essential for almost every project you do.

Transparent 12" ruler with smooth edge; a **steel ruler** and a **metal edge** for cutting against with a mat knife.

Mat knife or X–ACTO knife. It is impossible to cut thick board with anything else, except a guillotine. You should also cut onto a **cutting mat** or **board**. A sure, steady hand is a must when cutting with any type of knife. A **retractable mat knife** is safer and the blade tip should not be at all blunt, or cuts will become frayed and untidy. A **longer-bladed kitchen knife** is needed to cut the puppet's head in half. Always ask an adult or teacher for help when cutting with knives.

Scissors should be very sharp to the points and suit the size of the job.

Small scissors are best for cutting around difficult shapes. Pinking shears are good for fancy edgings such as for the crepe strips around the sunflower's center.

Library paste is still made by some who prefer it to **cellulose paste powder**. It is made in minutes and is ideal for papier–mâché and light paper sticking.

PVA glue can be used in two different ways; undiluted, use it as a glue and diluted as a varnish. It is irreversible when dry.

Double-sided tape is clean, fast, and effective. It has been used in the lampshade project.

Paper gummed tape is cheaper than clear cellulose (Scotch) tape which cannot be painted over easily; **masking tape** can be. **Masking tape** is also very good for holding work down on your work surface, and can easily be peeled off without causing any damage.

Contact paper or **clear tacky-backed plastic** preserves delicate artwork like the pressed flower bookmark on p.60.

Brushes of five different sizes and shapes are needed for gluing or

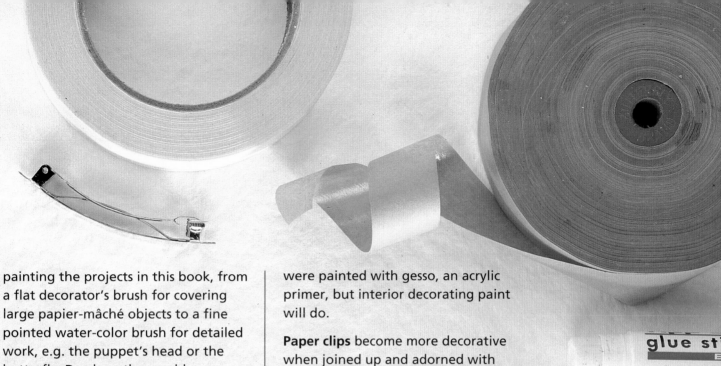

painting the projects in this book, from a flat decorator's brush for covering large papier-mâché objects to a fine pointed water-color brush for detailed work, e.g. the puppet's head or the butterfly. Do clean thoroughly, especially straight after gluing.

Paint is often used to cover the papier-mâché. Larger things, like the vase,

were painted with gesso, an acrylic primer, but interior decorating paint will do.

Paper clips become more decorative when joined up and adorned with colored tape.

Waterproof ink is permanent and is used to paint the papier–mâché cat mask.

SAFETY FIRST

The projects are fun to do, but as you work, keep the following in mind:

- ☞ Remember that you must always be very careful with sharp knives and pointed instruments. Ask an adult to help you when you need to cut out shapes with a craft knife.
- ☞ Be careful about leaving knives, scissors, and needles lying around when you are working – they could be dangerous to your younger brothers and sisters. Put a piece of cork on the end of your craft knife to protect you from cuts.
- ☞ If you have made a model that needs to be baked in the oven,

ask for help. It is no fun being burned, so always use an oven mitt putting things in the oven and taking them out again.

- ☞ When you have finished for the day, clear away all the materials you have been using and put everything away, making sure that all your knives, scissors, needles, and materials are kept in a box, safely out of the way.
- ☞ At the end of the day, wash your paintbrushes and clean any brushes and containers that have been used for glue or varnish.
- ☞ Store any oven-bake and air-dried clay that you have not used in an airtight container so that it is ready for next time.

Techniques

Paper Sculpture

Origami. The Japanese art of folding paper seems almost the simplest way of transforming paper in this book. The paper starts flat but quite soon it can stand up as a penguin or a placecard, jump like a frog or float like a waterlily.

The important thing to remember is to fold as accurately as possible and press hard along the fold with the back of a fingernail.

Pop-up Cards. Templates are included here to help you. The pig pop-up made on page 90 is not the usual incised type that open up to 90° to show a change in the inside shape (as in the larger pig face on the template on page 90.)

The butterfly card is an example of using double slits which make it hang within the framework of the card.

Start with an easy project, like this airplane.

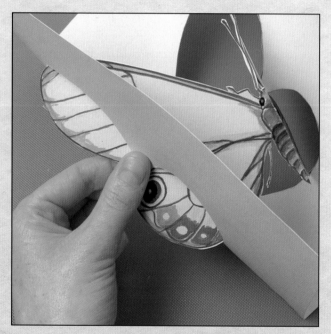

This butterfly almost moves through the card.

Accurate folds are essential for perfect shapes.

Tearing, Cutting, and Weaving

Handmade paper will tear and fold in any way, as the fibers lie in all directions. However, when paper is manufactured and formed along a belt, the fibers all lie parallel to the way of the flow. This becomes the way of the paper's grain. Rolling, folding and tearing are made easier in that direction. However, to make interesting zigzag shapes (for a card or the eyeshade), tear off pieces across the grain. To make the straightest tear possible, lay a ruler in the direction you want your tear. Then pull up the free paper sharply, cutting it against the ruler.

Tearing zig-zag shapes for the eyeshade (page 46).

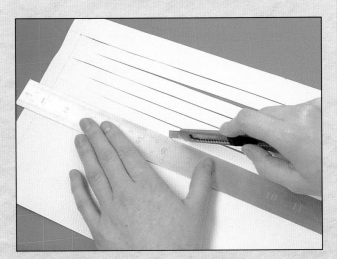

Always take care when using a craft knife.

Cutting with various tools has already been discussed on page 8–9. You will certainly have plenty of practice with straight cuts in the **Tearing, Cutting, and Weaving** section. Have fun with the "stained glass" project, although cutting the framework may need extra care.

Découpage

We use a type of découpage, meaning in French "cutting up", when cutting out pictures from magazines or photographs and using them as decoration on something else. Gift wrap pictures are cut out when decorating boxes. Postage stamps, which are usually already separate, are stuck down to form an interesting colorful pattern over the plain brown letter holder. Lastly, make use of your collected pressed flowers, grouping them together on card as a bookmark covered with clear matt tacky–backed plastic, or stick them down inside a piece of embossed card to make a simple and attractive greeting card.

Try several découpage arrangements before sticking.

Marbling

This is a beautiful age-old method of decorating paper. By the simplest method, Sumi Nagashi Gami – ink-marbled paper in Japanese (pictured below) – we use waterproof inks. Just take an ink-painted brush and touch the water's surface. Overlapping colors expand differently. Blow or push around, then lay on the paper.

Another marbling method to try involves using oil paint thinned with turpentine. The colors are stronger, but so is the smell, so make sure the room in which you are working has an open window for good ventilation.

A third, more complicated method takes much longer than the first, uses a carraghean moss size bath and other strange things, but the results can be wonderful. Some ready–printed marbled papers are being produced as gift wrap.

Try to keep the paper as flat as possible.

Papier–Mâché

Newsprint is recycled here to make attractive objects which can last for a long time. It can be layered with glue over a small tray, a balloon or chicken wire to transform it into three dimensions. You can mold some great things. For example, we have made a mask and a vase. Lastly, model a clown's head in modeling clay and copy it in papier–mâché. You could make several from one head!

Allow the object to dry between layers.

Butterfly Card

This might look difficult, but it is easy if you can trace off the template.
You can make up different colored designs for different people.

YOU WILL NEED

- Pale gray card, 11¾" x 8¼"
- Mat knife or small scissors
- HB pencil
- Paints and a fine brush
- Template (see page 91)

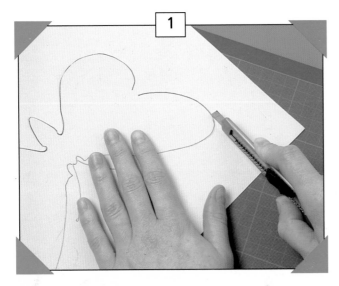

1 Find butterfly template and trace and copy onto card. **Then cut out carefully around the outline stopping at fold lines at sides.** You could fold the card in half and cut with scissors carefully around the head, antennae and legs to fold half way round the wings, after cutting again from tail to fold.

2 Draw in more details with a pencil.

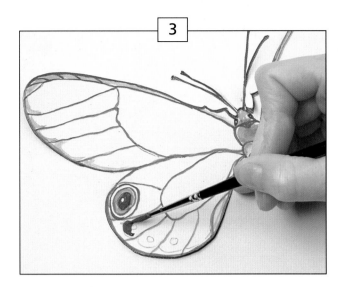

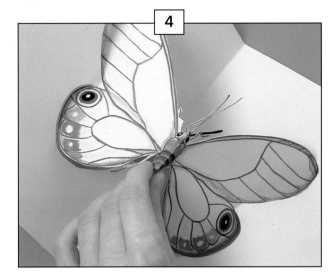

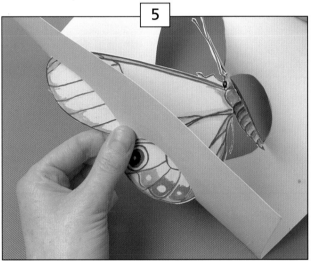

3 Color with paint. This butterfly is a Windowpane butterfly, but you could choose another kind.

4 Pull out butterfly from center fold and reverse its middle fold.

5 Press forward at side folds, mid-wings. See it almost suspended in flight! You can stick another piece of card over the back of the butterfly if required.

Piggy Invitation

How could anyone refuse this pig? The nose is the greatest attraction.
It could not be made easier with the templates on page 90.

YOU WILL NEED

- Yellow card, 11¾" x 4⅛"
- White card, 3" x 2"
- Pink sugar paper, 5" x 3½" two pieces, each 6" x ½"
- Pig template (see page 90)
- HB and colored pencils
- Scissors
- Glue-pen or another glue with a brush
- Pen

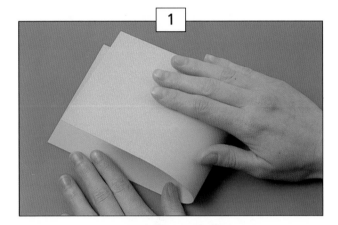

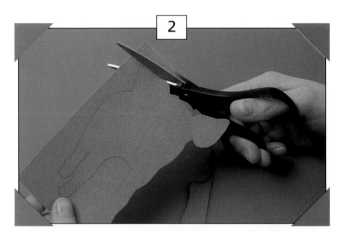

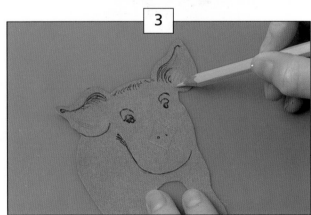

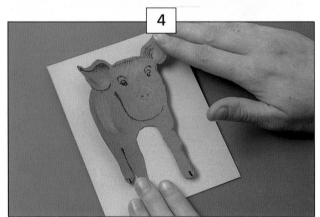

1 Fold length of yellow card in half and turn it round to open up from the bottom.

2 Having traced the template, drawn onto the back and redrawn it onto pink paper, **cut it out with scissors.**

3 Using colored pencils, draw in pig's features except the snout, some hairy highlights plus shadows underneath.

4 Put glue on the back. Then stick pig centrally onto yellow card.

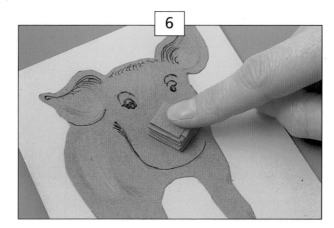

5 Take the two strips of pink paper each 6" x ½". Cross over the ends and fold one over the other alternately, until they are completely interlocked in a stack (sometimes called a Jacob's Ladder).

6 Stick the top ends together. Then glue and affix the bottom to the middle of the pig's head to form the snout.

7 Letter your invitation on a 3" x 2" white card. Glue it under the end of the snout.

8 Draw in the nostrils, ear holes and eyes with a pen. You can even add a curly tail at the back if you like, by cutting round inside a 1" pink circle until the center is reached.

Airplane

A rectangle of paper makes a very swift glider in a few easy steps.

YOU WILL NEED
- Rectangular paper, e.g. ⅔ of a square piece

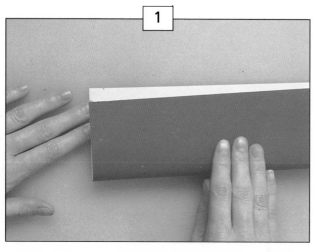

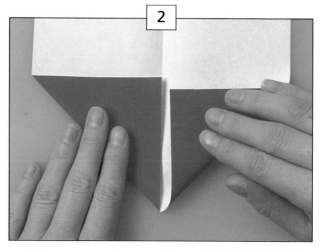

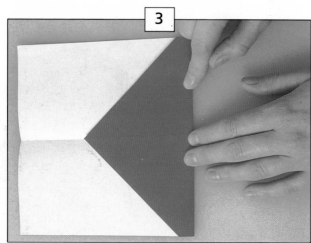

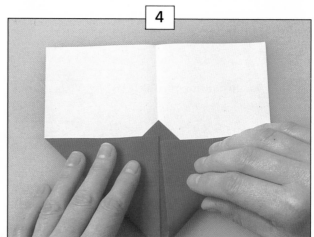

1 Fold the paper in half lengthways and unfold.

2 Fold bottom right and left corners up to meet along middle fold-line.

3 Leaving a small gap above flaps, fold bottom point straight up and over to meet middle fold-line.

4 Fold bottom right and left corners in to meet middle fold-line.

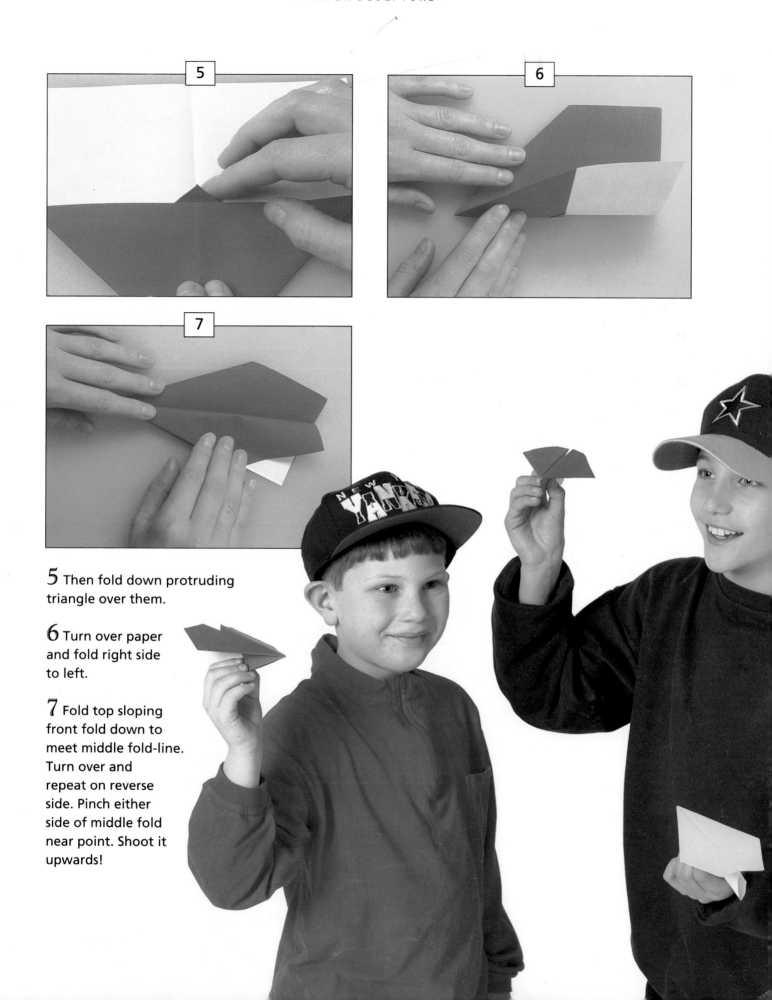

5 Then fold down protruding triangle over them.

6 Turn over paper and fold right side to left.

7 Fold top sloping front fold down to meet middle fold-line. Turn over and repeat on reverse side. Pinch either side of middle fold near point. Shoot it upwards!

Yacht

ORIGAMI

Blow these yachts along, and have a race with your friends! They make a colorful sight where ever they go.

YOU WILL NEED
- Square paper preferably colored one side only

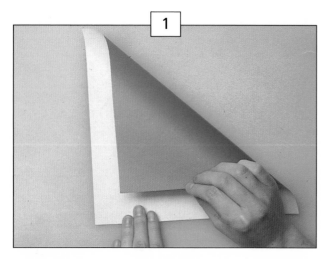

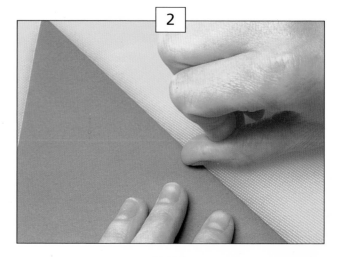

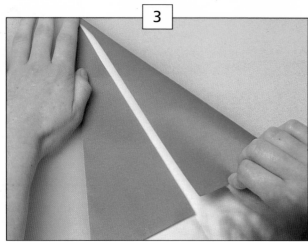

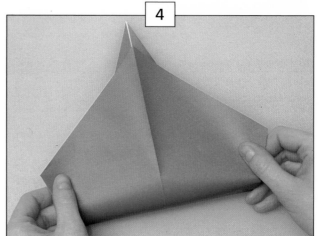

1 With white side on top, diagonally fold one side to other and unfold.

2 Remember to fold sharply right from the beginning with the back of your nail.

3 From top point, fold sloping sides with side points meeting at center fold-line to make a kite base.

4 Fold in half from bottom to top.

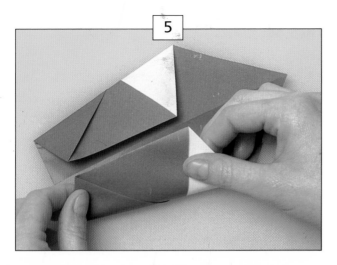

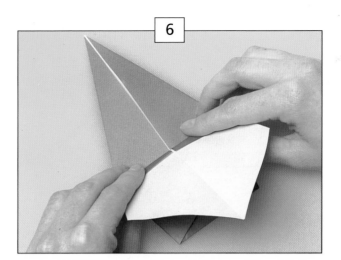

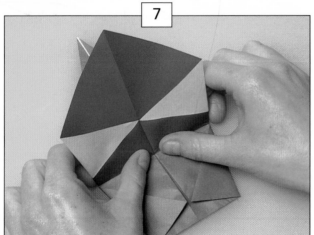

5 Fold sides in to meet middle fold-line.

6 Take topmost layer from point and fold downwards as far as possible.

7 Fold top layer upright, making a sail.

8 Curl the long point upwards. Now, blow it along from behind. Wow! You could make a race with some friends!

Sailboat

ORIGAMI

Send one in the mail to cheer a sick pal, or simply use as a gift tag, or place card.

YOU WILL NEED
- Square paper, preferably colored one side only

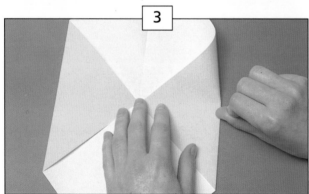

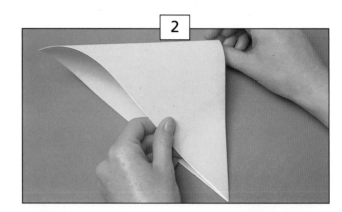

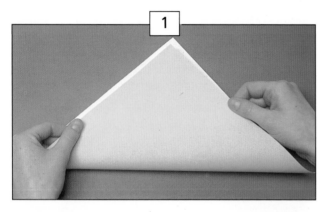

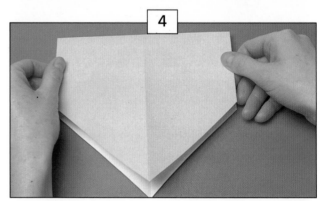

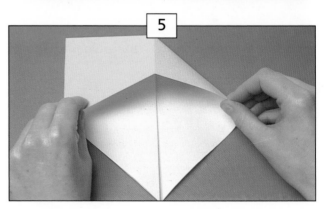

1 With square turned diamond way up, and white side up, fold in half from bottom to top.

2 Fold this in half sideways.

3 Press and then open flat again. Press opposite side points to middle.

4 Then fold top to bottom.

5 Now fold in half, along crease, open at the right side and squash flat.

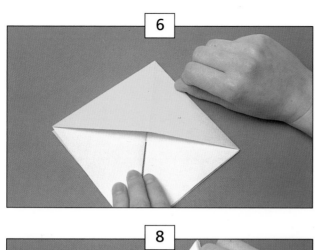

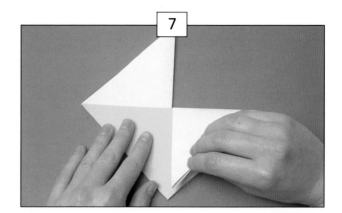

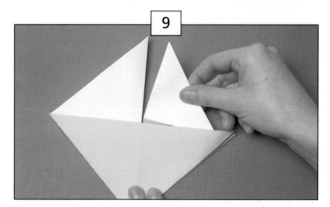

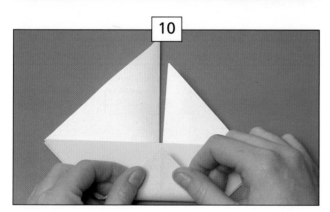

6 Turn over and repeat Step 5 on other side.

7 Turn paper around and bring top right point down to bottom point.

8 Then fold up again making a pleat.

9 Tuck this inside boat.

10 Bring bottom point up to middle and fold down to make a stand. You could use this as a gift tag or place card.

Penguin

ORIGAMI

Just plain black and white, but it looks so smart. Soon make a family
or even a flock of all different sizes.

YOU WILL NEED
- Square paper, black on white

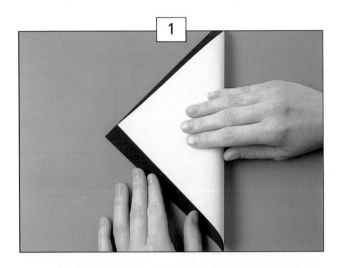

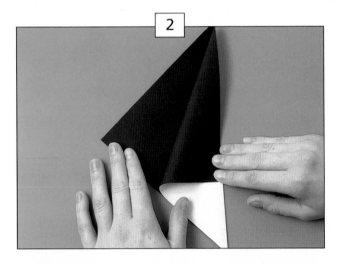

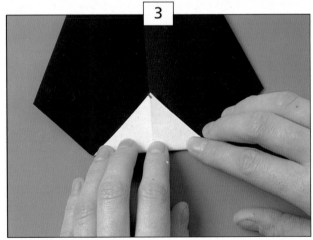

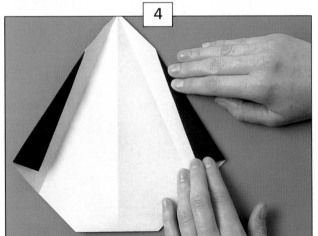

1 With square turned diamond way up, and the black side on top, fold paper in half from side to side.

2 From top point, fold top layer over to meet folded side. Turn it all over and repeat step 2.

3 Open flat backwards, black side uppermost, and fold up bottom point to make a tail.

4 Turn over and fold under middle points equally each side, up to a third of the way from top, as shown. Then fold in sides again to meet in the middle at top.

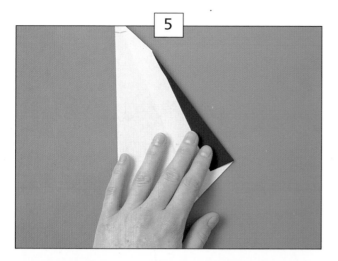

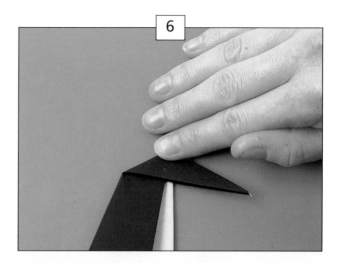

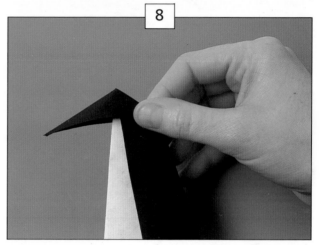

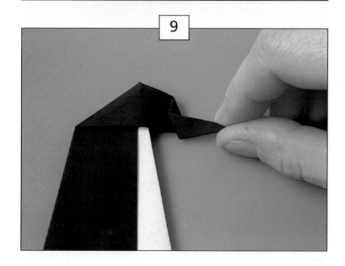

7 Pull up top again.

8 Pressing thumbs together at peak of last fold pull down head, reversing its fold.

9 Press down beak three quarters of the way up, making equal slanting folds to one side and then the other. Then pull beak end up again making similar folds just under the last. Opening the middle of beak and pinching the end, push it in and then squeeze flat each side.

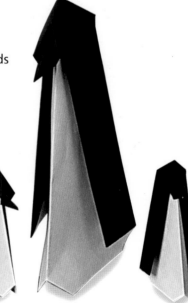

5 Fold backs together.

6 Fold top point forward to one side then the other, making slanting folds down towards back.

Mobile

Make these colored decorations for a nursery mobile. The balloon forms the first stages of the goldfish.

YOU WILL NEED

- 2 squares of paper, each a different color
- Needle and cotton
- Two strips of foamboard or cardboard 15" x 1½"
- Pen or pencil

PART ONE

BALLOON

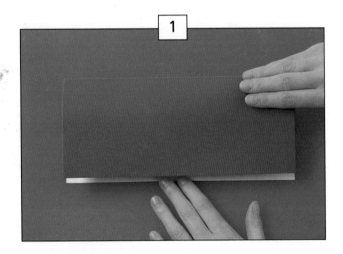

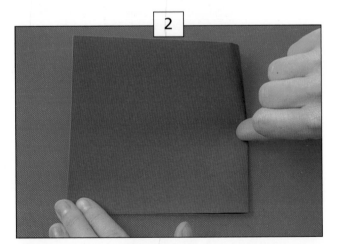

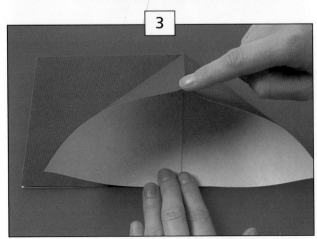

1 Fold first square in half from top to bottom.

2 Then fold from side to side.

3 Lift top half along fold-line and start opening to make a triangular shape which is pressed down—a squash fold!

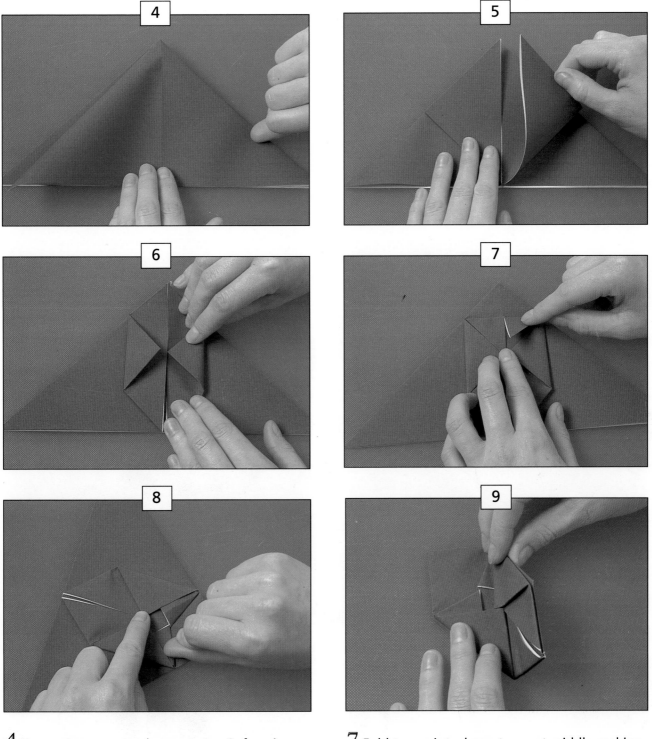

4 Turn paper over and repeat step 3, forming a shape called the waterbomb-base.

5 Fold top bottom points up to meet top point.

6 Bring top right and left side points to meet in middle.

7 Fold top points down to meet middle making 2 flaps.

8 Direct these flaps into pockets next to them and press. Turn paper over and repeat steps 5 to 8.

9 Fold right corner up and over diagonally.

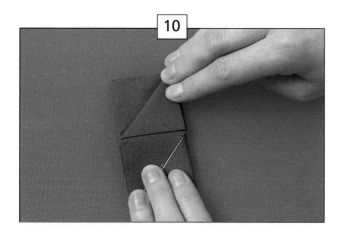

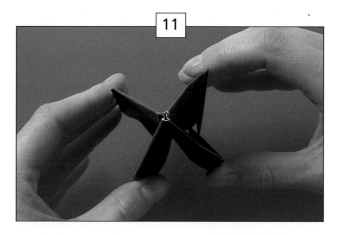

10 Press flat and unfold. Repeat steps 9 and 10 with left side.

11 Holding loosely, blow into small hole at base. Your inflated balloon can be hung from a mobile or a Christmas tree using a needle and cotton.

PART TWO

GOLDFISH

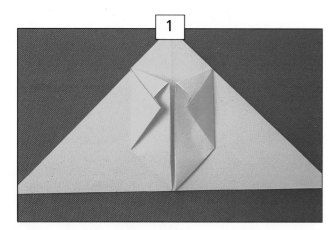

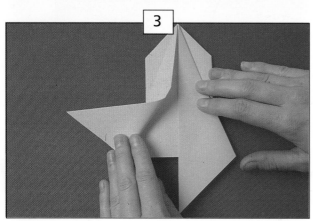

1 Fold as far as step 8 of the balloon on page 27.

2 Turn over paper. From top point, fold right and left sides sloping down to meet along middle fold-line.

3 Fold left bottom point up and outwards to about half way up as shown.

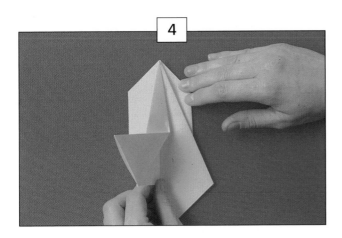

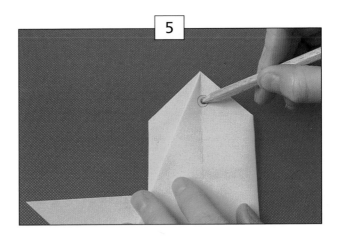

4 Press left-hand top layer all over to right side.

5 Then draw eyes either side of the head. Finally, thread cotton through the top of tail fin so that it can hang as a mobile. Now, holding the paper loosely, blow gently into small hole at base of tail. The inside should gradually inflate.

To assemble the mobile see instructions on page 37.

Jumping Frogs

It is interesting for frog-lovers everywhere to see how they can jump or somersault.

> **YOU WILL NEED**
> ● A fine light weight square of frog-colored paper e.g. 8″ sq. = 2″ frog, 10″ sq. = 2½″ frog etc.

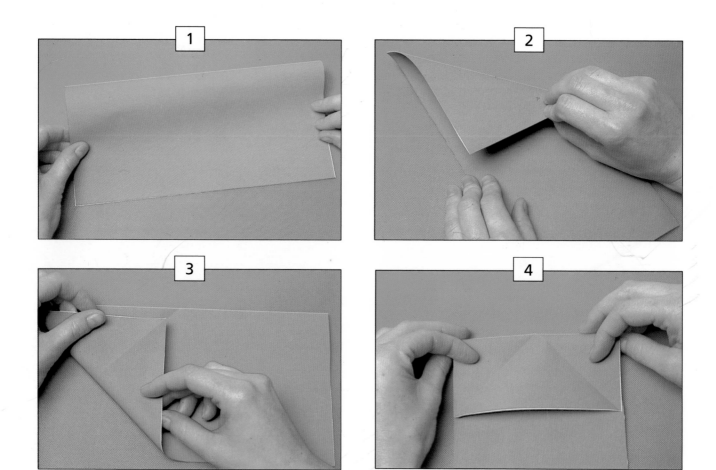

1 With white side facing up fold in half.

2 Fold over top right corner to lie level with left side. Press flat and unfold the corner.

3 Fold over opposite left corner to lie level with middle fold-line. Press crease and unfold corner again.

4 Paper is turned over. Then fold down top to middle, press and unfold.

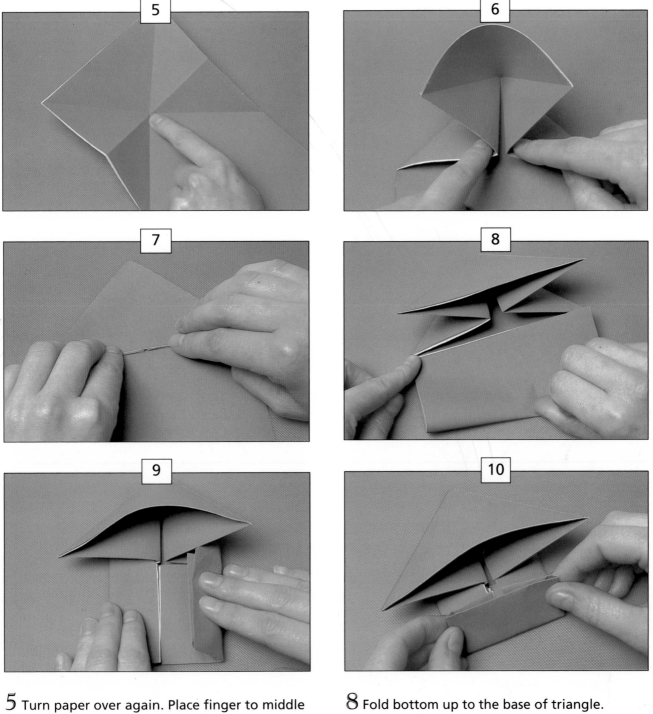

5 Turn paper over again. Place finger to middle of fold-lines. Push down. Then sides should pop up.

6 Place a finger each side at last crease across. Pull sides together and down towards you.

7 Press top down into a triangle.

8 Fold bottom up to the base of triangle.

9 Fold in sides under top triangle to meet middle.

10 Fold up bottom to meet base of triangle.

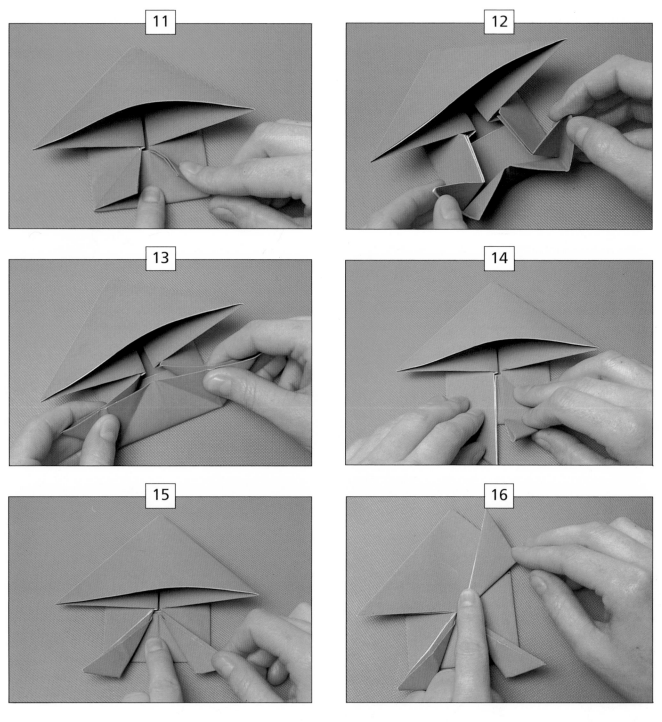

11 Fold top side corners of front flap down towards the bottom.

12 Holding bottom points of these flaps with thumbs, pull out middle points from behind with forefingers.

13 Stretch them to sides and press flat.

14 Fold lower side points down to middle bottom.

15 Fold back up twin bottom points as legs.

16 Fold up top triangle's bottom points as arms.

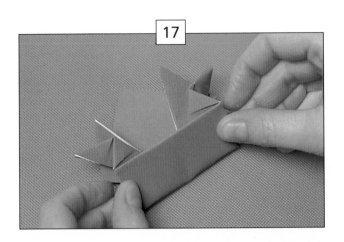

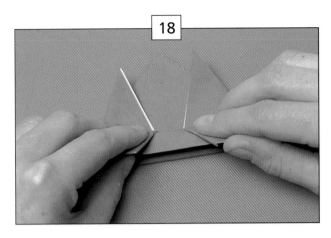

17 Fold up bottom section.

18 Press down bottom section in half, making a pleat.

19 Turn over complete frog. Press and slide a finger down its back. It should jump, even do a somersault! Have fun!

Crane Mobile

You must be experienced enough by now to make this fine set of birds!

YOU WILL NEED

- Square paper e.g. 10" squares in five assorted colors
- Needle and cotton
- Two strips of foamboard or cardboard, 15" x 1½"

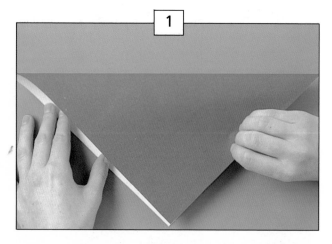

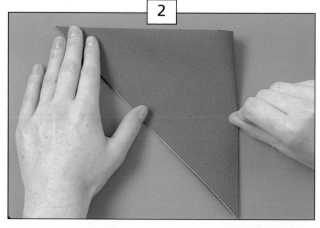

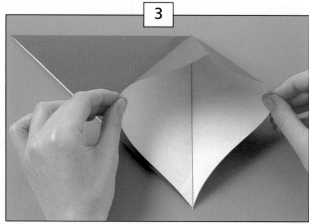

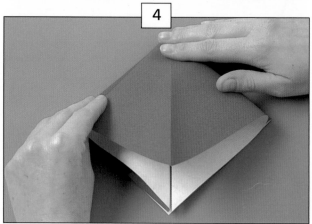

1 With a square turned diamond way up (white side on facing up) fold top to bottom.

2 Fold this in half sideways right to left.

3 Lift top layer along middle fold, opening paper out.

4 Then squash flat to make a diamond with that. Turn paper over and repeat steps 3 and 4 from reverse side—you have reached preliminary base.

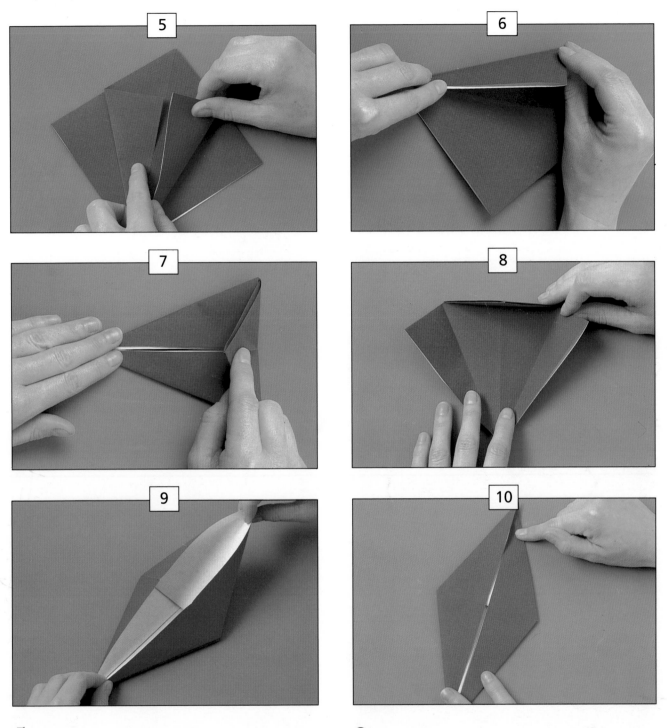

5 Now fold left and right top layer open edges to meet middle.

6 Turn over and repeat step 5 on the other side.

7 Fold down shorter top triangle.

8 Unfold left and right layers from under top triangle.

9 Lift the bottom point up and continue lifting until side edges meet in middle. Press paper flat making diamond shape. Turn paper over and repeat steps 7, 8 and 9.

10 You have now reached the bird base.

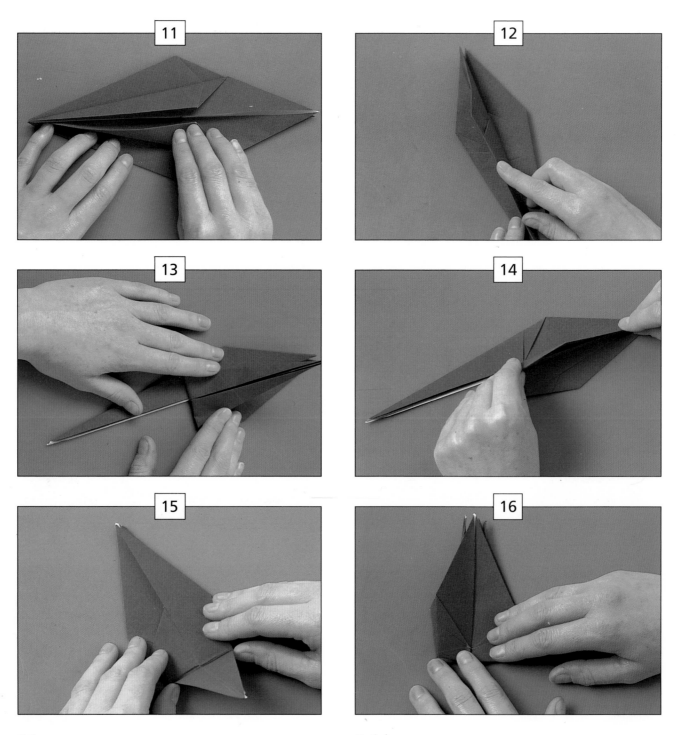

11 Taking the right side of the top layer, fold edge in to meet middle line, repeat on the left side. Turn over and repeat. The two top points will later become the crane's wings.

12 Fold top right layer over to left.

13 Bring top layer of bottom point up to meet top of crane's wings.

14 Fold top left section over to right. Repeat step 14 on the other side.

15 Then step 13.

16 Fold top right section over to left.

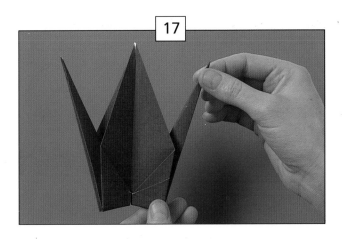

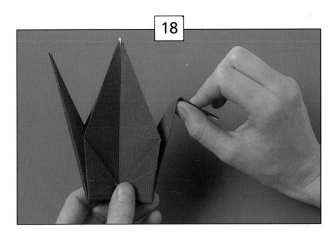

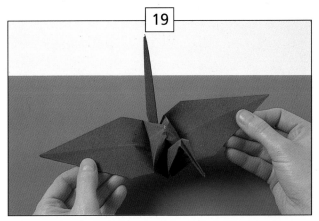

17 Pinch bottom points tightly and pull the top points outwards.

18 Place thumb into fold of right point with finger on top, to pull point down inside itself to make head.

19 Fold down wings and pull gently apart to open body.

TIP

☛ When you have enough cranes to form a mobile, take a sharp needle and thread cotton through the tops of the cranes' backs. Cut two strips of foamboard, or cardboard, with slots ¾" deep x the thickness of card. Thread bottom cross-strip with two cranes in the center, one above the other, plus one either side, nearer ends. The top cross strip just has one each end. It is more interesting to hang each crane at a slightly different level.

Animal Faces

These are very easy to make and can be used as finger puppets, or just to make a table-top display.

YOU WILL NEED

- Square paper—whichever color is appropriate e.g. a pig in pink
- All-purpose glue—quick drying

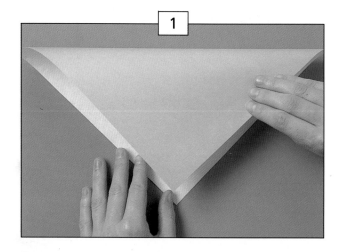

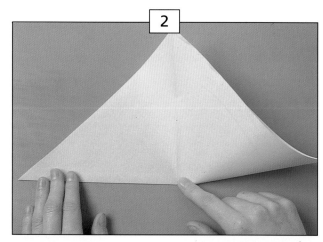

1 With square turned diamond way up and color face down, fold and unfold from top to bottom.

2 Then fold and unfold it in half again having turned the paper round.

3 Bring bottom corner up to meet middle and press.

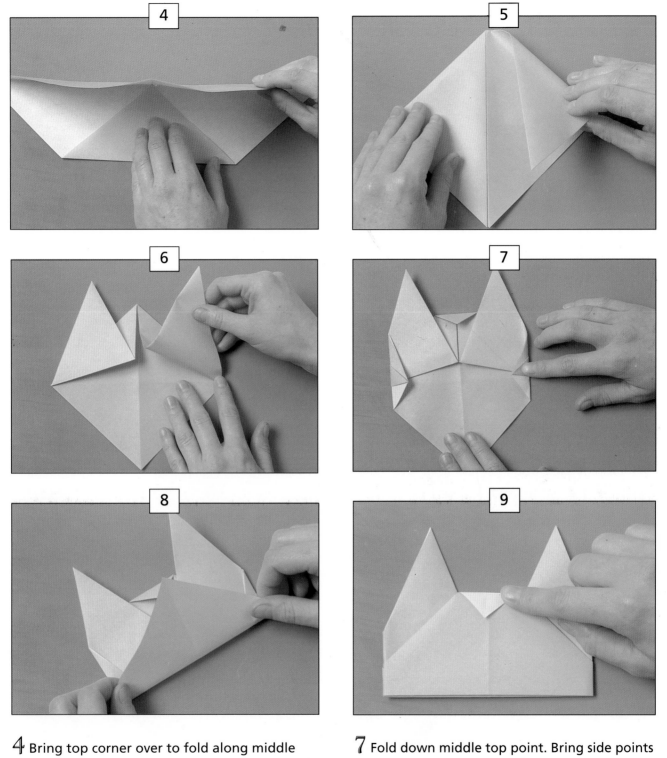

4 Bring top corner over to fold along middle line.

5 Top side points are folded down to meet at bottom point.

6 Then fold the points back up as shown.

7 Fold down middle top point. Bring side points in at an angle and press.

8 Then fold bottom point up to bottom of ears.

9 Turn paper over and fold middle point down.

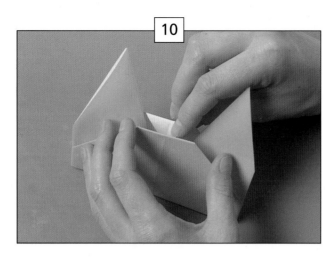

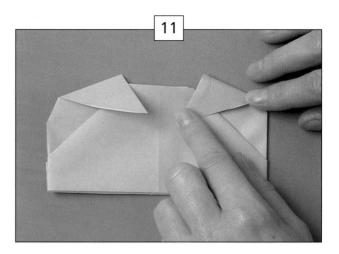

10 Tuck it in between front and back layers and glue it for a finger puppet. Use this shape for a fox or cat and bring the sides in more at step 8 for a rabbit. For a dog, fold the ears down and outward.

11 The pig's ears are bent down and folded inwards. For a frog, fold ears down and inwards. Then, lift again, open sides and press down flat as a diamond shape. For a bear, fold the frog's eyes up in half.

Life-like Sunflowers

SCULPTURE

The finished flowers will make all your efforts worthwhile. Then if you make the papier mâché vase on page 80 you can really show them off.

YOU WILL NEED

- Tracing paper, 1 piece 6" sq. and 1 piece 10" x 5"
- Templates (see page 92)
- 3 lengths thick crepe paper, 6" x 27" in dark and pale yellow and pale green
- dark yellow, brown & black crepe paper, pinked or fringed, ½" wide x 18"

- 2 lengths yellow tissue paper, 6" x 27"
- Brown corrugated card, ⅜" wide x 36" and 2" x 1½"
- Pale green crepe paper, 12" x 2½", and 8 or 9ft. x ¾"
- Leaf green crepe paper, 10" x 5"

- Wire approx. ⅛" diameter x 33" long
- All purpose glue – quick-drying
- PVA
- Needle and cream thread
- Ruler, pencil & scissors— regular or pinking shears

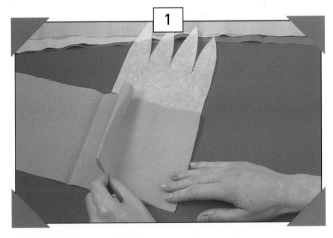

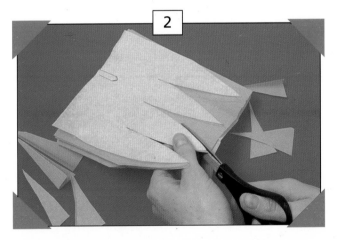

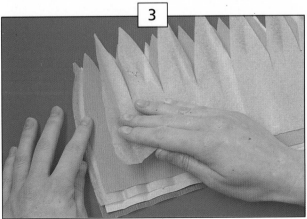

1 Find the template patterns. **Trace these and cut out. Fold up, concertinawise, and cut lengths of yellow tissue and yellow and green crepe papers to the width of template.**

2 Draw around petal shapes only. **Then cut them out.**

3 Layer together strips of petals, unfolded, with pale green on the bottom, then pale yellow crepe, yellow tissue, darker yellow crepe and one yellow tissue on top.

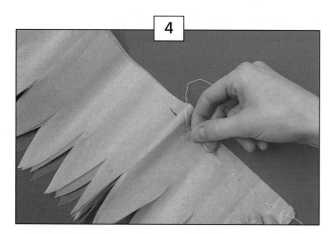

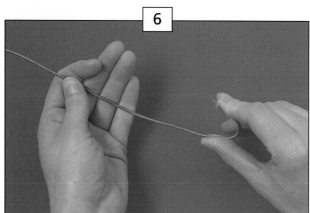

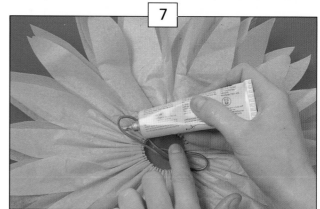

4 At the beginning, with needle and thread, fasten by oversewing and knotting firmly, making running stitches ⅜" from the bottom edge.

5 Join up ends, overlapping slightly. Hold thread end and gather up the papers as tightly as possible, so that the ends form a circle and leave a ½"–¾" diameter hole in the centre. Oversew end stitches together and cross over in the middle twice.

6 Take wire and bend over bottom end 1" on itself to make it safe. Then the top is gently curved over 90°, starting 6" down, and poked through the center of the flower.

7 Twist the end pushed through, into a flat loop or figure of eight, against the flower. Stick it to the petals with quick setting all purpose glue, holding firm until set.

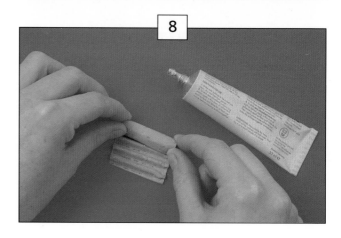

8 Roll up, with glue, 2" x 1½" piece of corrugated card.

TIP

☛ The crepe paper can then be formed into petal and leaf shapes by finally stretching it with thumbs and curling the ends by pulling them gently over a pencil stem.

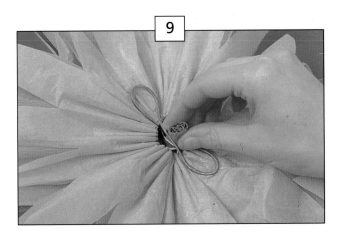

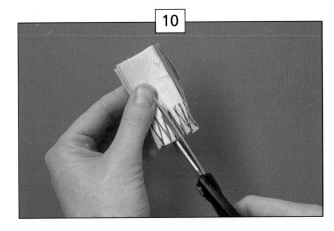

11 This is dabbed with PVA, and bound around the back of the flower, over the protruding corrugated card.

12 Follow on likewise over to wire adding on glued ¾" wide strip. Wind this strip round the wire. At a slight angle below the flower level, wrap in a prepared crepe leaf-green shape and, after a few inches, another one. **On reaching base of stem, bind back up over 1", cut and stick down firmly.**

9 Stick it halfway through the center of the flower with some glue. Make sure the wire still curves out of the flower.

10 Having traced the calyx template take the pale green 12" x 2½" strip and, folded concertinawise to template width, cut out calyx.

13 Dab with glue and roll ½" wide black crepe strip, pinked or fringed, along top edge, around corrugated roll in flower center.

14 Add 12" of corrugated ⅜" strip plus 18" of ½" brown crepe strip and more brown corrugated.

15 Intersperse with fringed ½" wide dark yellow crepe. Finish center off with dark brown corrugated until 3½" in diameter.

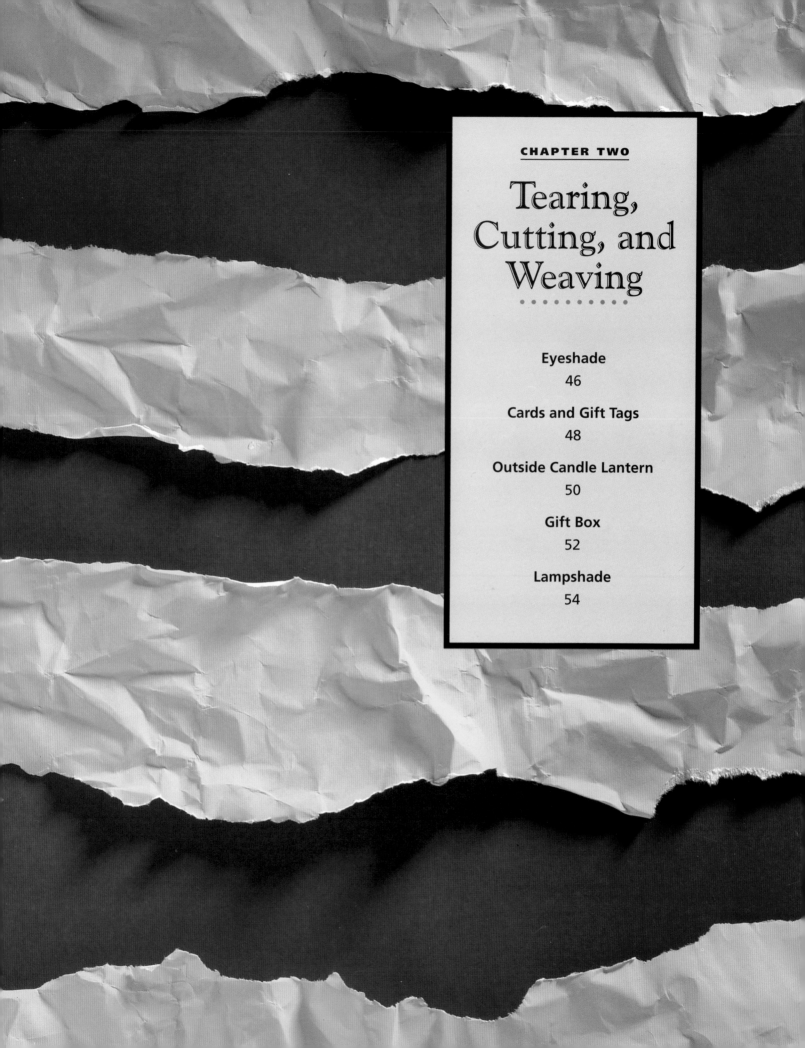

Eyeshade

Make this eyeshade for those long, hot summer days in the garden.
It's fun to make and will always keep you cool.

YOU WILL NEED

- 4–sheet board (or thick card), 26" x 4"
- Thin scrap paper in complementary colors, e.g. glassine, tissue and bank paper
- Ruler (or tape measure)
- Pencil
- 14" string
- Scissors
- Glue stick or similar dryish paste

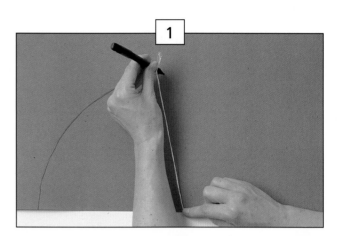

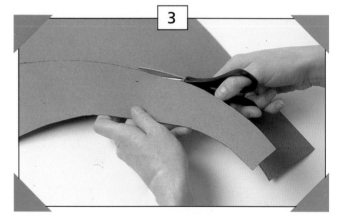

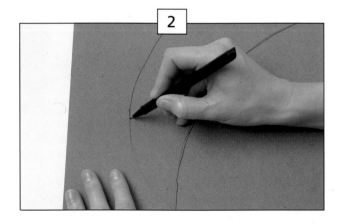

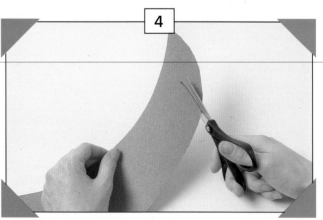

1 Tie one end of string around the pencil. Then, with a measured length of 9" on the string, hold the end without the pencil at the center of the long edge of card. Stretch the pencil end out and draw a semi-circle with the 9" radius. Re-tie the pencil on the string at 13" long and lightly draw another circle around the first.

2 With a free hand gradually taper both sides of the last semi-circle to meet the first, making one end pointed and the other blunt.

3 **Cut out the shape with scissors.**

4 **Make slots in shade on the opposite sides at either end.**

= 46 =

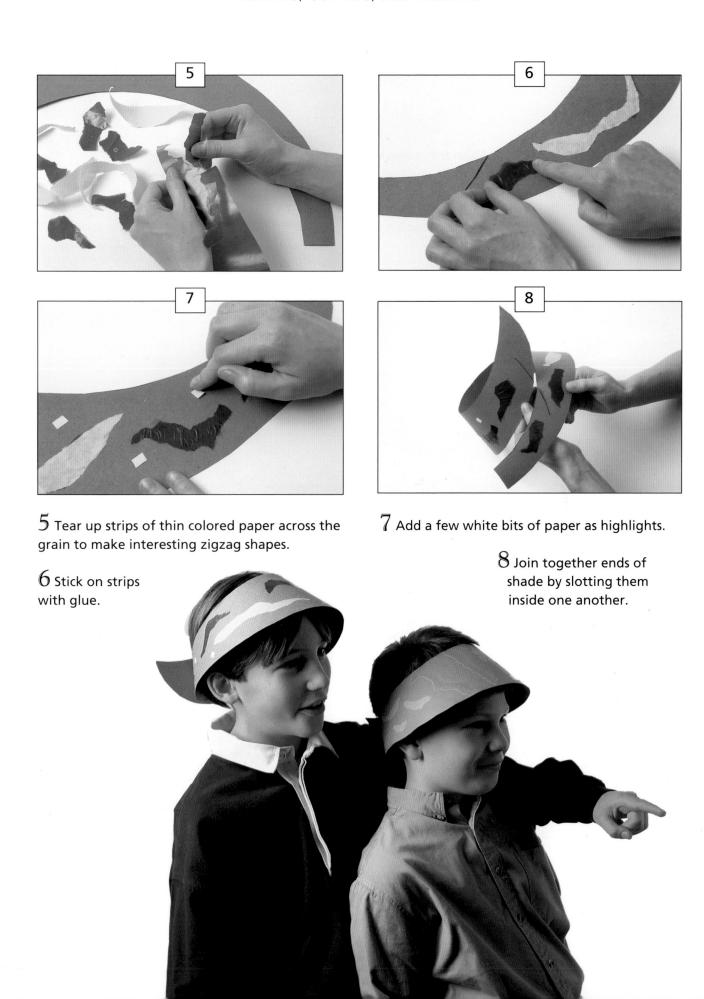

5 Tear up strips of thin colored paper across the grain to make interesting zigzag shapes.

6 Stick on strips with glue.

7 Add a few white bits of paper as highlights.

8 Join together ends of shade by slotting them inside one another.

Cards and Gift Tags

· ·

TEARING

This involves folding and tearing shapes from tissue, to make simple or intricate patterns. Overlay a contrasting colored paper to complement a present.

YOU WILL NEED
● Purple construction paper
● Yellow tissue paper
● Glue stick

TIP
☛ **Glue sticks** and **glue pens** are handy when only a little is needed.

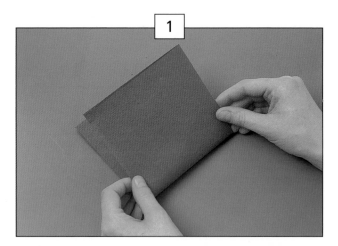

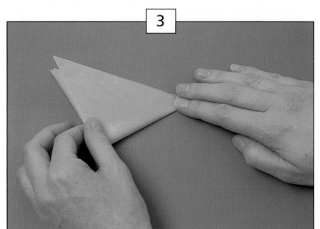

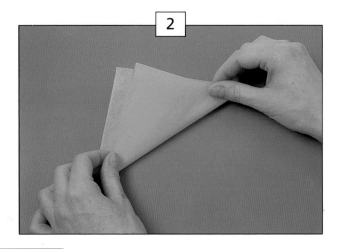

1 Take the purple paper and fold it in half. Fold it in half again, across the first fold.

2 Fold the yellow tissue paper so that it matches the folded purple paper as it is. Then fold over the tissue from corner to corner.

3 Then again fold corner to corner.

4 Tear out some interesting shapes from the folded sides, not the edges.

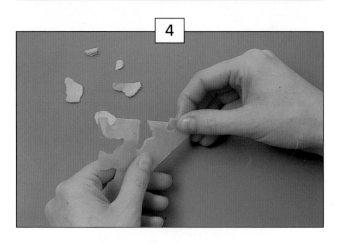

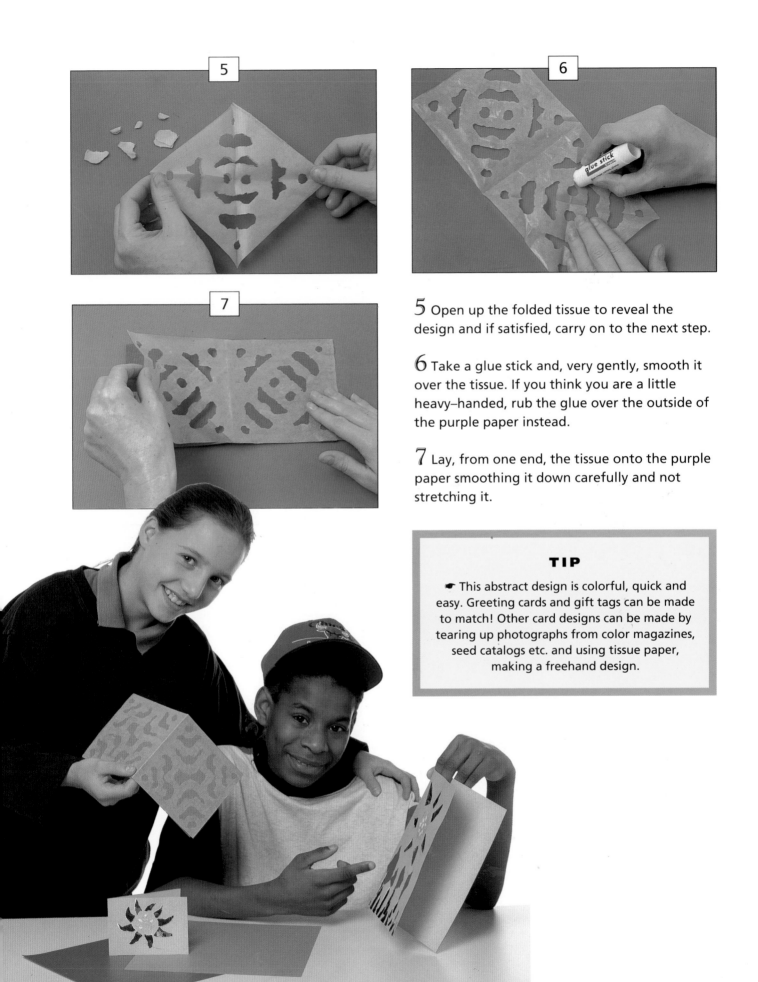

5 Open up the folded tissue to reveal the design and if satisfied, carry on to the next step.

6 Take a glue stick and, very gently, smooth it over the tissue. If you think you are a little heavy–handed, rub the glue over the outside of the purple paper instead.

7 Lay, from one end, the tissue onto the purple paper smoothing it down carefully and not stretching it.

TIP

☛ This abstract design is colorful, quick and easy. Greeting cards and gift tags can be made to match! Other card designs can be made by tearing up photographs from color magazines, seed catalogs etc. and using tissue paper, making a freehand design.

Outside Candle Lantern

With a stained glass effect from cut-out windows covered with colored tissue, this makes a very attractive garden lantern.

YOU WILL NEED

- White or colored metallic card, 9½" x 4½"
- Tracing paper
- Colored tissue papers e.g. orange, pink, pale and dark blue
- Double-sided tape
- Ruler (metal)
- Mat knife and cutting mat
- Scissors
- Pencil
- All purpose solvent-free glue
- Template (see page 93)

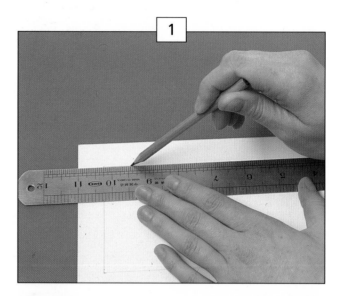

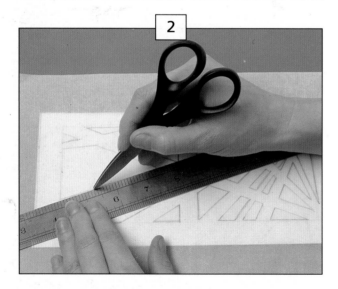

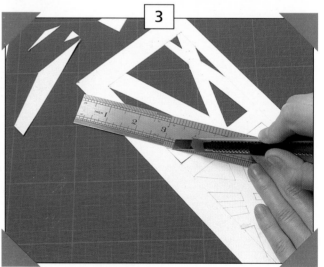

1 Draw ¾" margins around bottom and sides of card and ½" margin around the top.

2 Trace off the template and transfer it onto the card.

3 **Cut out the design with a craft knife and metal ruler on a cutting mat.**

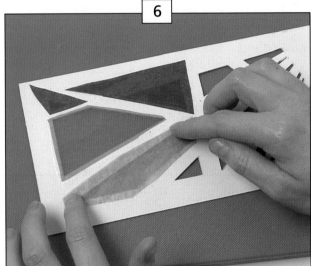

4 Draw around the shapes of the holes onto different colored tissues for the design.

5 **Cut out the shapes with scissors.** Remember to make each shape a little larger than the hole it is meant to fit.

6 Stick the tissue shapes in place with all–purpose glue around the edges. Make sure that you glue all of the shapes on the same side, so that no stuck edges are showing.

7 With double-sided tape (or other glue) join up the sides to make a cylindrical shape, which will fit over a night light.

Gift Box

Enjoy weaving these pretty little boxes. You could use them to hold a candle lantern, or an origami gift.

YOU WILL NEED

- Thin colored card, white on one side and black on the other, 16½" x 11¾"
- 6 colored art paper strips, 15" x ⅜"
- Pencil and ruler
- Mat knife and cutting mat and metal edge ruler
- Scissors
- Raffia, ribbon or string

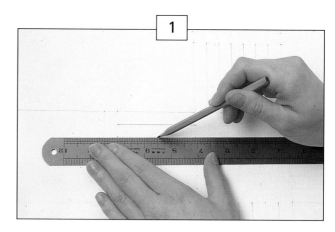

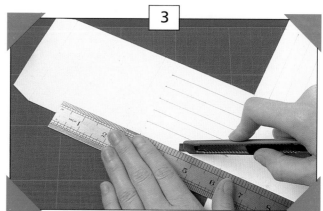

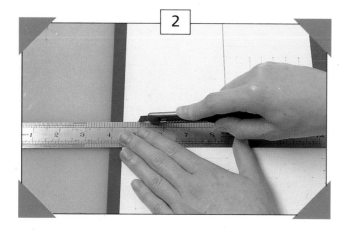

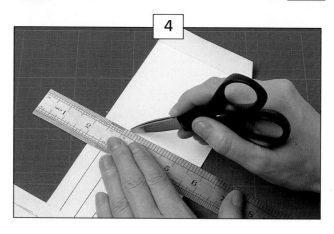

1 Trace the template for a 3½" 3D cube on page 94. Transfer the ouline to the back of your card, the white side.

2 **Cut around the outline of the box shape with a mat knife onto a cutting mat. You can also use scissors for this.**

3 **Cut out slits as drawn, ⅜" apart around each side. It is easier with a knife and ruler.**

4 Score along folding lines of flaps and around the base lines and corners of box, using the back of the scissor blades.

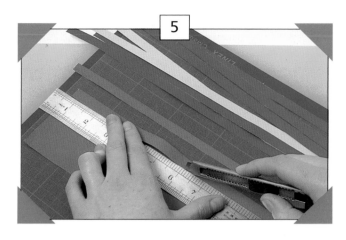

5 Cut strips of colored art paper 15" long x ⅜" wide if not already done.

6 Taking a strip at a time, weave it in and out of the side slits, gradually pulling up the sides and overlapping the ends. Work each row alternately so that a one–to–one pattern is formed. (After some practice, you can experiment making different patterns, with overlapping two strips instead of one sometimes.)

7 Assemble the box by creasing all sides, then fold and glue the tabs. After lining with tissue, filling and closing the box, tie it together with colored raffia, ribbon or string. An ideal holder to present a small gift like some pulp jewelry!

Lampshade

Amazing effects can be achieved by weaving strips of paper. The glassine paper used for one of these has a transparency, which is ideal for shining light through.

YOU WILL NEED

- Straight, cylindrical lampshade frame e.g. 6" diameter x 6" deep
- Sheet of opaque, white, strong, thin paper e.g. onionskin, tracing, wax paper trimmed to twice the height of the frame plus 4" by 1" longer than the circumference e.g. 20½" x 16"
- Sheet of colored or textured paper e.g. 20" x 8"
- Mat knife with cutting board
- Pencil, ruler and long metal straight-edge ruler
- 1" wide double-sided tape and/or glue stick (this is less strong)

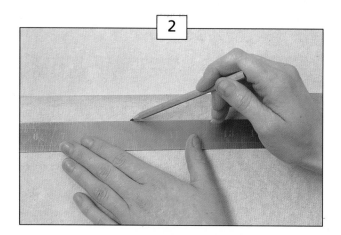

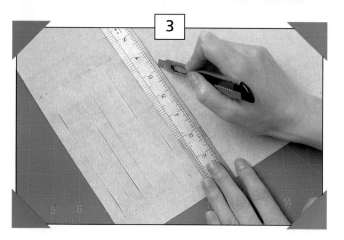

1 Fold opaque white paper in half along its length. Then open it up again.

2 Draw a line 1" below fold-line and another 6" below that (or depth of shade), leaving a space below that of 1". Mark along each line at ½" intervals, or to your choice.

3 **Then align and cut with mat knife on board, making slits 6" long.** Refold the paper the other way so the slit half is above the plain half. Take a sheet of colored or textured paper cut to size. Draw a line 1" from top edge of length. Then ½" from one side mark ½" intervals, or to your choice, to within 1" of bottom. Repeat on opposite side.

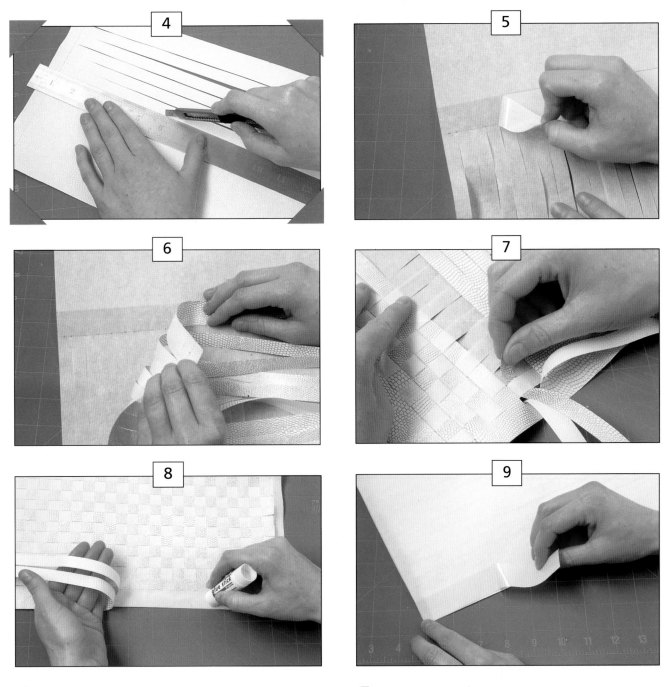

4 **Align marks with metal rule and cut to the end of one side and within ½" of the other.**

5 Place double-sided tape along top of refolded white paper.

6 Stick top 1" of colored or textured paper to it.

7 Then gently pick up strips in order and from top to bottom. Start weaving under and over white paper, keeping strips as close together as possible until 6" deep (or depth of shade.)

8 Stick bottom 1" strip to white paper.

9 Stick double-sided tape to top and bottom of the half of the white paper that has not been slit.

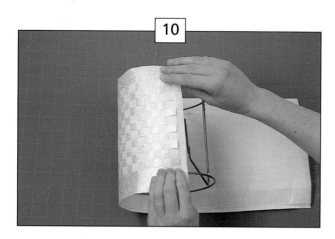

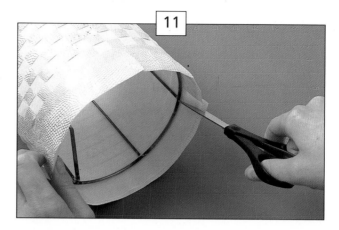

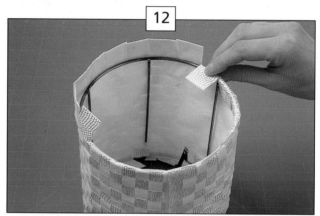

10 Wrap the whole length of weaving evenly around the lampshade frame.

11 Clip edges of paper standing above and below frame ¼" deep.

12 They will lie flat when folded inside and fit either side of the brackets which hold the bulb.

It is possible to weave a multi-colored version by substituting some different colored strips during the weaving process. One illustration shows a lampshade made with glassine paper, which is perfect for its transparency and color.

Pressed Flower Card

It is hard to match the natural beauty of pressed flowers. Arrange a permanent, impressive display for someone special.

YOU WILL NEED
- Hammer embossed card, 16½" x 11¾"
- Pressed flowers
- All purpose solvent-free clear glue or similar strong quick-setting glue

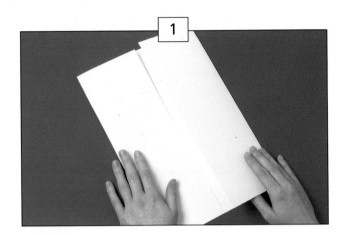

1 With card horizontal or landscape-way up, fold sides to the middle and unfold.

2 Arrange flowers to a pleasing arrangement in center section only. Pick stems up one by one and dab with glue to tack them into place.

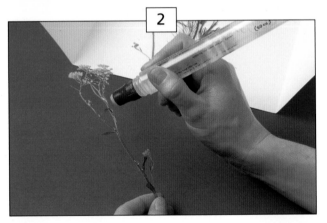

3 Carefully press them back into position and leave to set. Finally, the doors of the card are closed to keep the flowers protected.

Decorated Hinged Box

Choose a gift wrap that is decorated with clearly defined pictures and test your cutting skills with scissors.

YOU WILL NEED
- Clean, hinged box
- Pictorial gift wrap
- Scissors
- PVA glue and brush

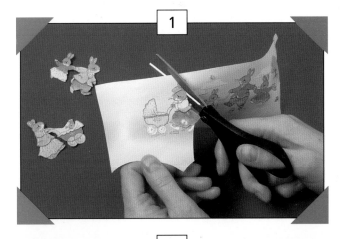

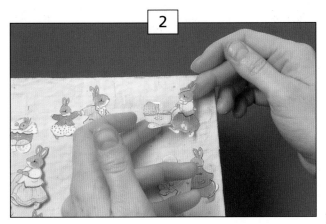

1 **Carefully cut out several pictures from the gift wrap.**

2 Try positioning them on the surfaces of the box in various designs until satisfied. Using PVA glue and a brush, stick pictures in places chosen, smooth down edges and leave to dry.

3 Varnish completely with diluted PVA. Leave to dry off and recoat at least twice for a waterproof, shiny finish.

Pressed Flower Bookmark

DÉCOUPAGE

Put a few small flowers and leaves down, cover with contact plastic film.
Hey presto! It's finished so quickly.

YOU WILL NEED

- Pressed flowers and/or leaves
- Tinted green pastel paper, 8¾" x 3"
- Contact paper (tacky-backed plastic film), 9¼" x 7"
- Scissors or mat knife and cutting mat

1 Arrange pressed flowers and/or leaves on the green pastel paper.

2 Peel back half of the plastic film from its backing sheet.

3 Slip the pastel paper onto the exposed backing sheet without disturbing the arrangement of flowers or leaves and within ¼" of the edge, making sure that it is straight.

4 Fold over the plastic film gently covering the arrangement.

5 Rub down the film to smooth out any air bubbles.

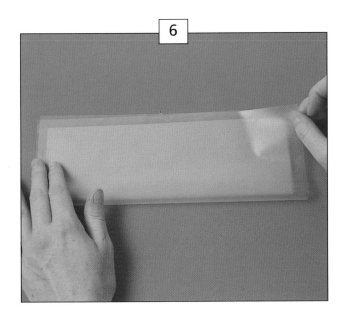

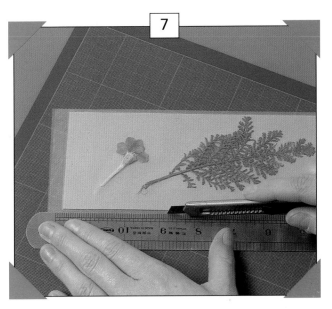

6 Turn over the whole holding it as straight as possible by the side and gradually pulling out the backing paper, cover the back of the bookmark with the rest of the film. Rub any air bubbles out smoothly.

7 **Trim with mat knife or scissors within ⅛" of the edges of the paper.**

Letter Holder

Use up some of your foreign stamp collection and make an attractive useful holder.

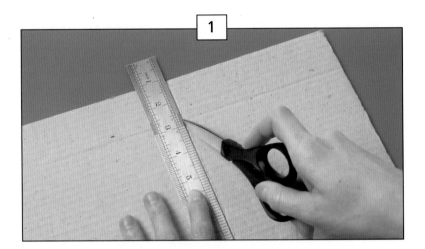

YOU WILL NEED

- Stiff card or rigid corrugated card, e.g. the kind used when packaging sheets or shirts— 13⅞" x 10"
- Brown wrapping paper or manila 2 x (7⅛" x 5⅞"), e.g. a piece of brown wrapping paper or 2 envelopes
- Foreign stamps – approx. 50
- Ruler
- Pencil
- Mat knife and cutting mat
- Scissors
- Hole punch
- Cord approx. 10" long
- Template (see page 95)
- Tracing paper
- PVA glue and brush

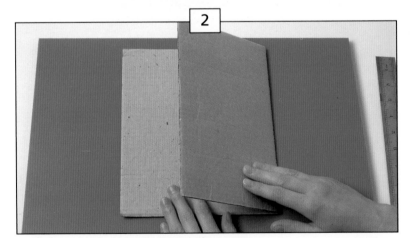

1 Score all the way across the stiff cardboard with the back of the scissor blades at 6" away from one edge.

2 Fold up the card along the same score line so that it is nearly double.

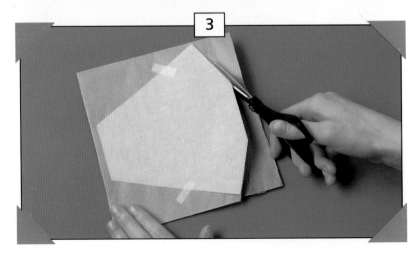

3 **Draw around template onto tracing paper, lay on brown wrapping paper and cut out two pieces.**

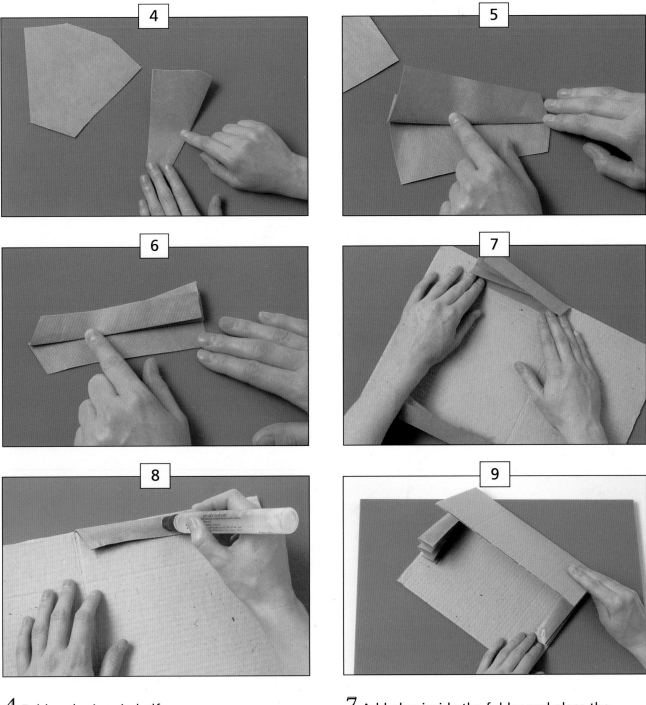

4 Fold each piece in half.

5 Then from the bottom points fold in half concertinawise.

6 Fold each side back the other way again to make the gusset flaps.

7 Add glue inside the folder and place the gusset pieces pointing down at the thinnest end to the bottom fold.

8 Put more glue on the top of the other gusset flaps.

9 Re-fold cardboard. Press the whole together and leave the glue to dry.

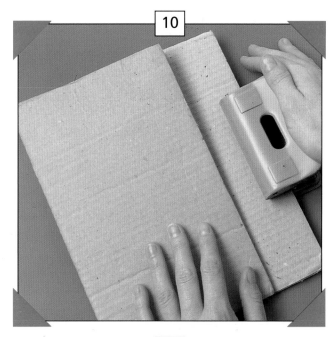

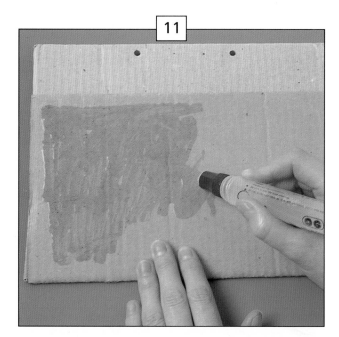

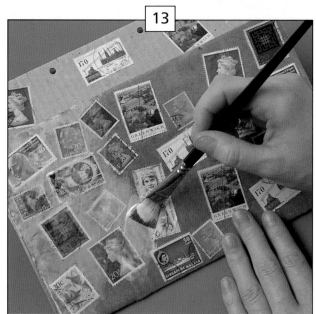

10 Take a hole punch (or you can carefully screw through with the point of a knitting needle or sharp scissors.) Make holes equally spaced either side of the center of the top of the holder.

11 Spread glue over the front of the holder.

12 Arrange stamps, leaving interesting shapes in between them, and place some straight along the top, missing the holes. Smooth down all edges.

13 Brush water-diluted PVA over the whole front. Dry and re-varnish for a better finish.

14 Knot cord one end and thread it through holes to make a loop in front.!

15 Tie a final knot at the other end. Hang it near the front door to put in your mail!

Fish Wall Hanging – Marbled Skate

MARBLING

The camouflaged pattern of a skate is mimicked by marbled paper.
Did you know that they had such interesting faces too?

YOU WILL NEED

- A wire clothes hanger, approx. 16" wide x 8" high
- A sheet of marbled paper of dark red and brown shades approx. 16½" x 12½"
- All purpose solvent-free quick setting glue
- Scissors
- Pencil
- String or strong yarn, minimum 15" long

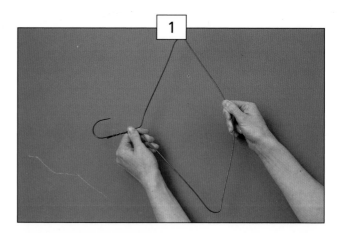

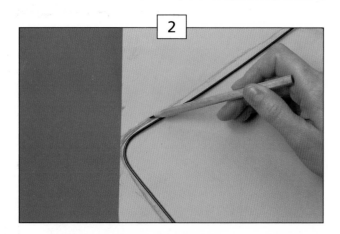

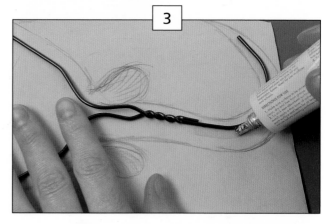

1 Hold top of hanger with one hand and the middle of the flat bottom of it with the other hand and pull apart until a diamond shape is formed.

2 Place re-shaped but flat hanger onto the back of marbled paper and draw around the outside of it.

3 Squeeze all purpose clear glue under the wire keeping it touching the paper. Then leave until set.

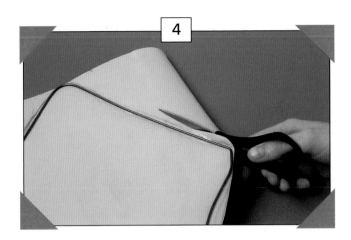

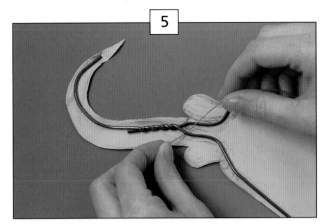

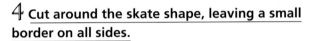

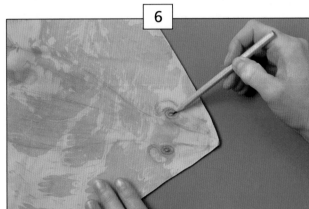

4 **Cut around the skate shape, leaving a small border on all sides.**

5 Thread string or strong yarn between any small gap under wire at each end.

6 Draw in eyes and shape of body and fins. Here is your decorative wall hanging!

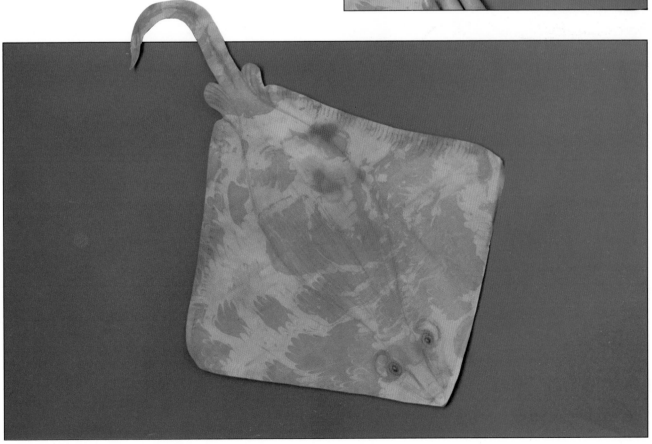

Marbled Stationery Folder

Make this to show off a sheet of marbling, covered with strong plain paper.
Use it to hold all your stationery.

YOU WILL NEED

- One piece 6 sheet board, approx. 21" x 13½"
- Three pieces cover paper, 15" x 7½", 22½" x 15", and 1½" x 1½"
- Two pieces marbled paper, 20¼" x 12⅞", 25¾" x 3"
- Metal cutting edge or ruler
- Mat knife and cutting mat
- Scissors
- Pencil
- Paste or glue and brush
- Compasses
- 1 paper fastener
- Pinking shears

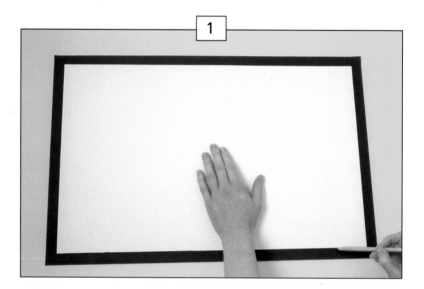

1 With board centrally placed on largest cover paper, draw round it.

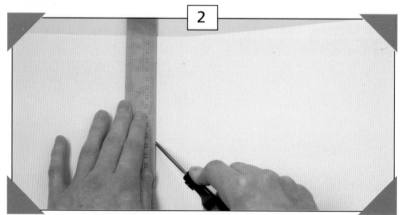

2 **With help from an adult, take just the board and score halfway through down the center with the knife. Then, score 1" to the left of center, and 9½" to the right of center, leaving 1" to the edge to bend up as a flap. Bend over at the middle too.**

3 Cover the work surface with a waste sheet, then seal the scored edges to strengthen with dilute PVA and lightly prime all over the board with the PVA, ending with the outside.

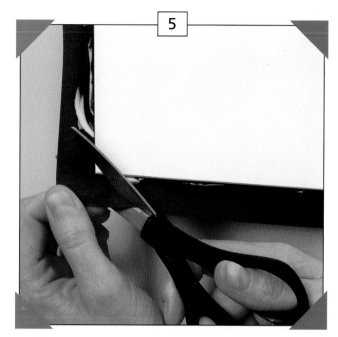

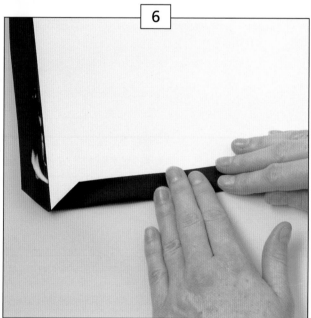

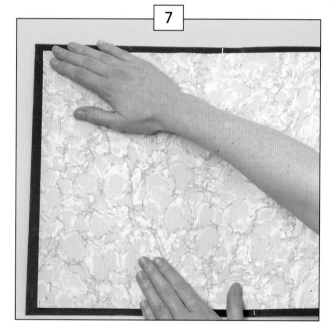

4 With a waste sheet still in place now spread paste all over the cover paper as quickly as possible before it dries.

5 **Lay the front of the folder on the cover paper, first leaving straight margins as marked before, cut across corners diagonally the thickness of board away at least. Then cut up to the board at folds when cover paper has been straightened over the back of folder.**

6 Paste over flaps and press them down firmly.

7 Now spread paste over the back of the largest marbled paper and lay over the inside of the folder. Leave to dry when smoothed.

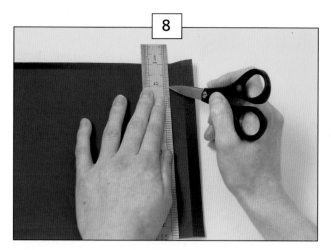

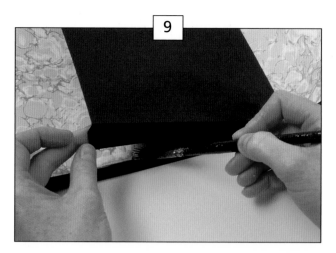

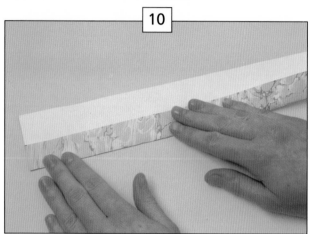

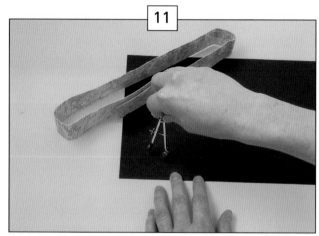

8 Take second size cover paper, meanwhile, and score ¼" inside one long edge. Paste, fold over and stick down to make a hem. Mark 1" inside shorter edges and fold against ruler. Then mark ½" inside from edges and fold in the opposite direction, concertinawise. Mark and score ½" inside other long edges and glue down flap at bottom of sides only.

9 Place this pocket inside folder and mark position, facing outward along center of side with the flap. Glue it down.

10 With long strip of marbled paper, make ¾" wide folds along a long ruler or straight edge inside the length of it so that edges meet along the middle and stick down.

11 Wrap this band around folder and make a hole with the end of scissors for the paper

fastener through both ends (1"–2" from the end approximately). Using the compasses, draw a circle 1½" diameter on remaining piece of cover paper.

12 **Cut around this circle with pinking shears.**

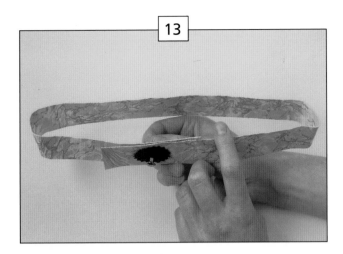

13 Make a hole through this circle to push through it the paper fastener and then that through the hole in the band.

14 Close and assemble the folder with the band.

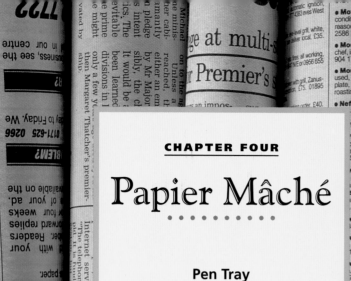

CHAPTER FOUR

Papier Mâché
· · · · · · · · · · ·

Pen Tray

LAYERING

This is a very simple papier mâché project, and a good one for beginners.
The pen tray is both fun to color and very useful.

YOU WILL NEED

- A shallow 8"–9" oblong tray
- Petroleum jelly
- Newsprint scraps over 3" long
- Wallpaper or cellulose paste, and brush
- Diluted PVA glue
- Complementary colored matt paper scraps and strips
- Scissors
- Wire cooling rack

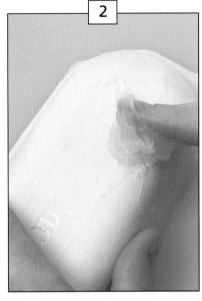

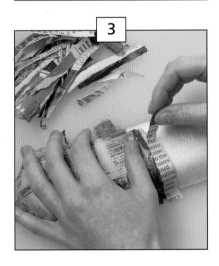

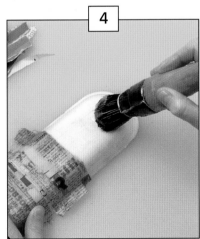

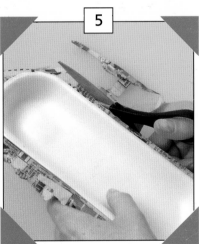

1 Mix up paste and leave to swell.

2 Thinly grease underside of tray with petroleum jelly. This will be your mold.

3 Tear newsprint into ½" x 3" strips and paste them across the tray overlapping slightly.

4 Perhaps use different colored newsprints to help count the number of layers, until eight have been completed. Leave to dry in a warm airy place, preferably on a cooling rack.

5 **With scissors, cut away rough edges to a smooth tray shape again, following around the mold.**

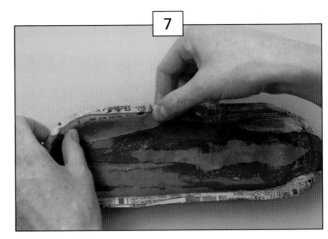

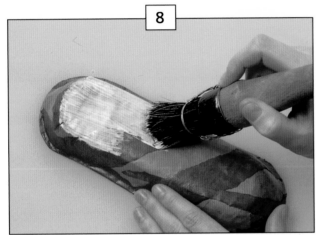

6 Remove mold, gently easing it apart at first. Wipe out excess grease from new shape with a tissue.

7 Take torn strips of colored matt paper that you have prepared and arrange and paste them down, pressing over edges and around the underside.

8 Smooth down edges all over and paint over the whole with diluted PVA for a protective coat. Dry and re-coat at least three times.

Clown Puppet

PAPIER MÂCHÉ

With lots to do, give yourself time to make this puppet well. It would make a gift for someone to treasure for a long time.

YOU WILL NEED

- 1lb modeling clay, any color
- Modeling tool
- Newspaper
- Very fine grade sandpaper
- White poster and gouache paints
- Paste brush and medium and fine paint brushes
- Wallpaper (or cellulose) paste
- Mat knife and kitchen knife
- Dilute PVA glue
- Wire cooling rack
- Templates (see pages 95–96)
- Yellow thin card, 5" x 3½"
- Green crepe paper, two pieces, 9" x 8"
- White crepe paper, 2" x 2" and 3" x 36"
- Needle and white thread

1 With strips of modeling clay from a 1lb slab, build and compress a block about 4" x 3".

2 Build-out eyebrows 1½" down from top, ears at the sides (from the level of the eyes down to the level of the mouth). Use a modeling tool for putting in finer details like the eyelids and rounding off the big nose and large lips.

3 Having mixed the paste and torn the newsprint in tiny ½" pieces, brush the paste over the head and dab over the bits of newsprint working all around the head. Make 8 layers like this and leave for 48 hours to dry in a warm, airy place on a wire rack.

4 **When dry, cut with a kitchen knife all round the head in a straight line across it.**

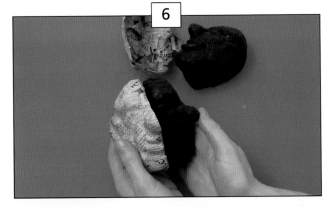

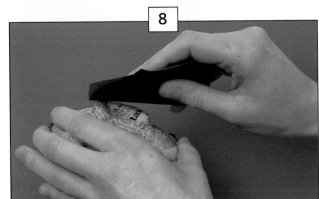

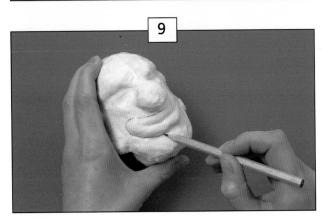

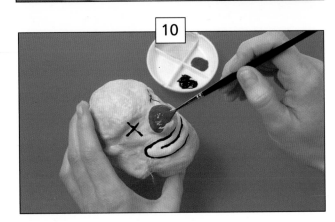

5 Now you have two halves.

6 Loosen around inside the edges with the tip of a mat knife and then holding the papier–mâché firmly, gradually drag out the modeling clay half-molds. If you are careful enough, you can save these, press them together and re-use them.

7 Fit the papier-mâché halves together again. Paste strips of newsprint across the joins, overlapping all round. Leave in a warm place again to dry for a few hours.

8 Rub down any rough edges with fine grade glass-paper. If you want to add more to the facial features, do it now and dry it again.

9 Then paint all over it with white poster, process white or gouache paint. Draw around some of the features, mouth, eyes and nose with a pencil.

10 Then mix and paint over all except the lips with pink paint. Next outline the mouth and put black crosses on the eyes. Lastly color the nose red and leave to dry quite hard.

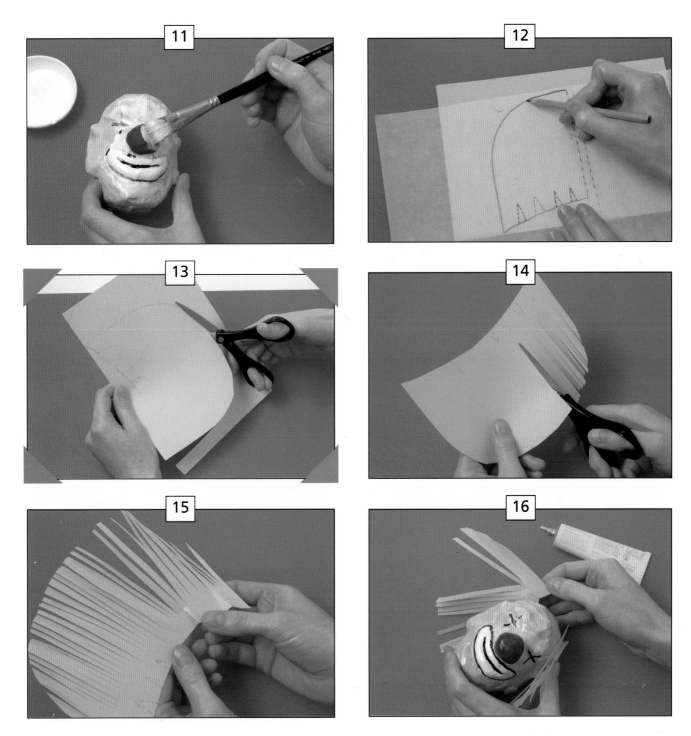

11 Brush over the whole head with diluted PVA as a varnish.

12 Trace off the templates for the clown's hair, dress and mitten.

13 **Cut out the hair's shape in yellow thin card.**

14 Fringe the card from the bottom, up to ¼" margin along the top.

15 Pleat the top edge as indicated on the template.

16 Stick it into place around the back and sides of the head.

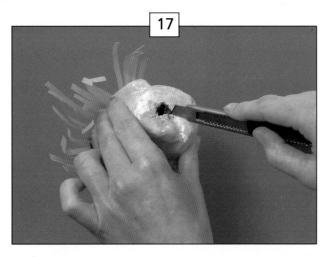

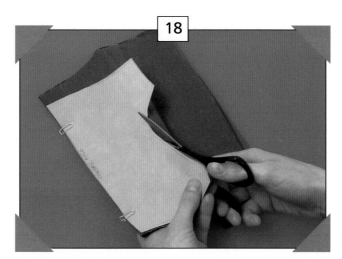

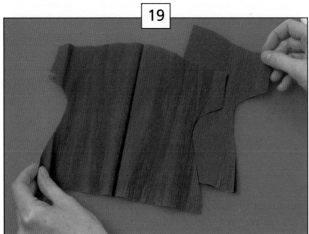

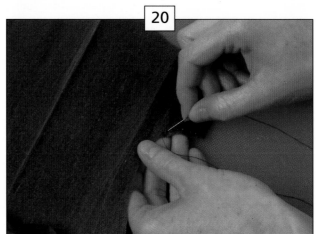

17 Open up the neck, enough for a finger to fit inside.

18 **Cut around the shape of the dress from the green crepe paper, first folding the crepe paper in half. Remember to place the straight edge of the shape along the fold of the paper, and cut through both layers along the other edges. Repeat with the other piece of green crepe paper.**

19 Open up the pieces and place one on top of the other.

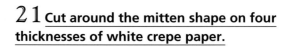

20 Baste together down the sides and along the shoulder seams with the needle and thread. Then oversew with back stitches.

21 **Cut around the mitten shape on four thicknesses of white crepe paper.**

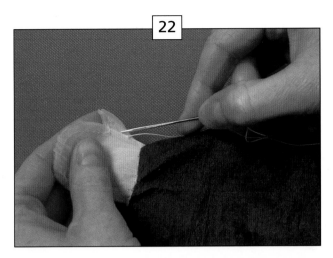

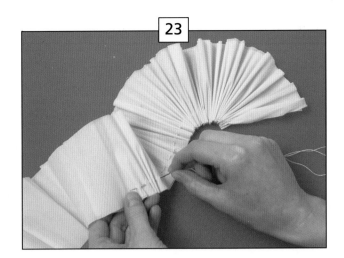

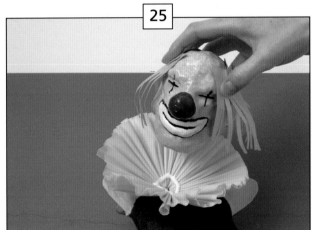

22 Baste these together into two mittens, using tiny stitches, or if you have access to a sewing machine, get the clothes all seamed up by this. Then sew the mittens to the sleeves of the dress.

23 Take the long white crepe strip and with a needle and thread make running stitches ¼" from bottom edge.

24 Gather up the crepe into a ruff and join up the ends overlapping slightly. Push inside the neck of the dress and stitch and glue together. Then add PVA glue to the top of ruff.

25 Press on the head and leave until dry.

Vase

· ·

A large vase is just what is needed for the sunflowers on page 41 and will display them naturally. Keep it plain or decorate with torn paper.

YOU WILL NEED

- Chicken wire, 18" x 36"
- Binding wire or soft wire, 24"
- Newsprint
- Very fine grade sandpaper
- Gesso or white interior decorating paint
- 2" paint brush
- Wallpaper (or cellulose) paste
- Cardboard tube
- Waterproof PVA adhesive (optional)

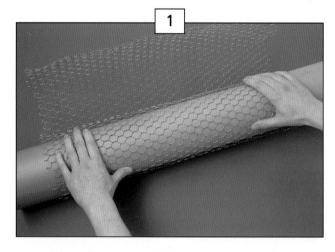

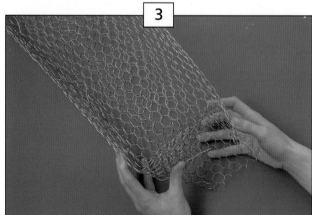

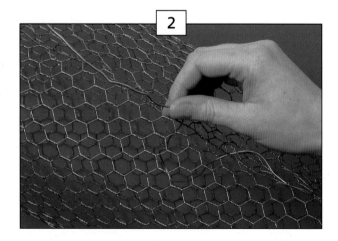

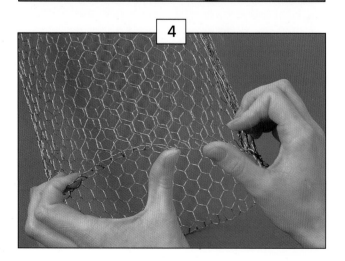

1 Bend the chicken wire round into a cylinder, rolling out any wrinkles with the cardboard tube.

2 Join the two overlapping edges together with soft wire by weaving it through the holes.

3 At one end bend over the edges to overlap in the middle a little. Pleat them up and flatten by pressing them down on a firm base.

4 Fold over about 1" at the top so that there are no sharp points. Make a lip around the edge by bending it out.

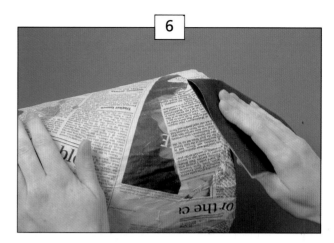

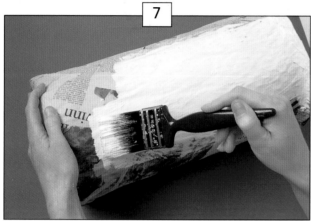

TIP

☛ **Wire cutters** are essential for cutting chicken wire.

5 Tearing the newsprint into wide strips, start pasting it around the outside with the brush. Always overlap. Cover the outside of the chicken wire frame with four layers of newsprint, using different colors for each layer. Allow to dry, then paste four more layers on the inside of the frame.Dry again and paste a further four layers on the outside. Dry on a rack in a warm place for 48 hours.

6 Sand down any rough edges or creases with the fine sandpaper.

7 Paint over the inside and outside and leave to dry again thoroughly. This is a nice big vase to hold your sunflowers.

Cat Mask

Surprise your friends by wearing this mask. It will take a week to make,
but will last for years.

YOU WILL NEED

- Round blown-up balloon
- Petroleum jelly
- Newsprint
- Wallpaper (or cellulose) paste and brush
- PVA glue
- Thin strong card, e.g. waste packaging
- 2 letter (or bulldog) clips
- 2 staples and stapler
- Scissors or mat knife
- 12" black hat elastic
- India ink
- Paint and brush

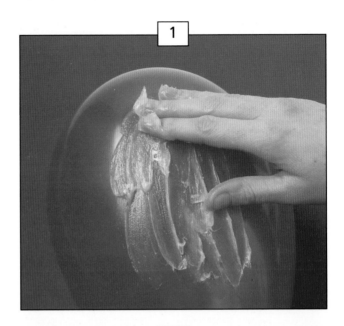

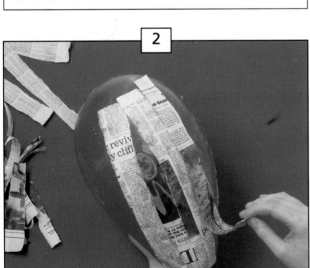

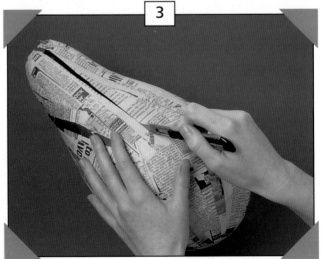

1 Smear petroleum jelly thinly over all the balloon.

2 Having mixed paste and torn newsprint into narrow longish strips, paste them, overlapping, from top to bottom and all around the balloon eight times. As with the pen tray (see page 73), it may help to use colored newsprint to

distinguish between each layer and to make a note of the number you are on. Leave to dry eventually in a warm airy place for 48 hours.

3 **Cut through straight around the balloon shaped papier mâché. You may need to draw a line first.**

4

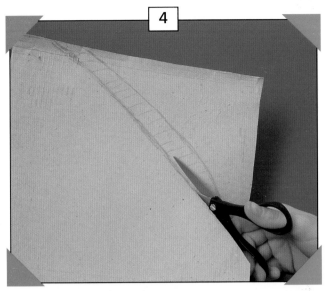

5

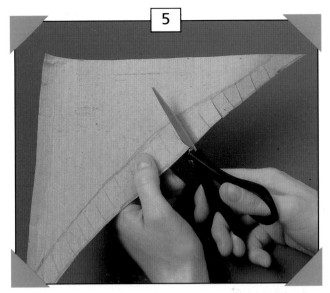

6

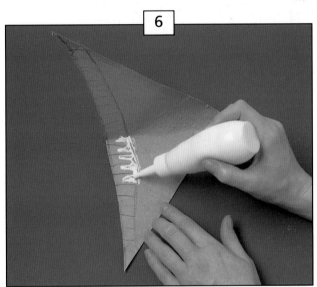

7

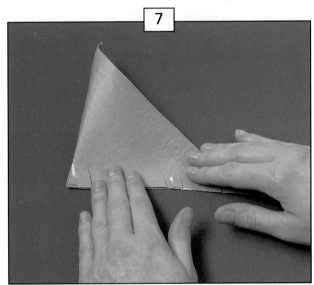

8

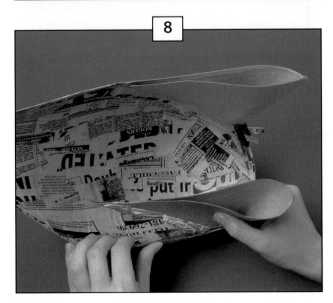

4 **Cut out two triangles from the thin strong card for the ears.**

5 **Cut into or flute the longer edges.**

6 Put PVA glue along these edges to half way.

7 Fold over the other halves onto these.

8 Place inside the top of each side of the mask.

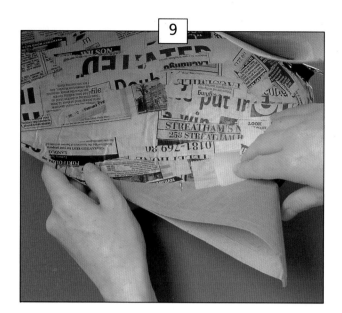

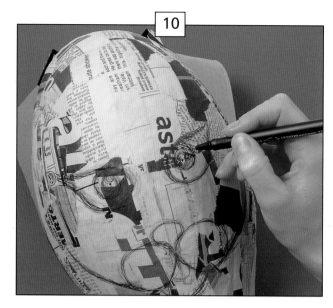

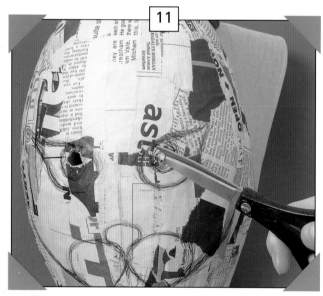

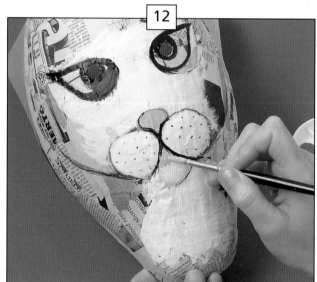

9 Fix in place with more PVA using more strips of newsprint if necessary and hold with a letter clip till dry.

10 Place mask over face and ask someone to plot from the side at what level and how far apart the eyes should be.

11 Remove mask and place on firm surface. Then, with the help of an adult, make two holes with a large needle or scissors and cut a small hole around each. Draw around each eyeball a cat-shaped eye equidistant from the center, and a nose with cheeks and tongue below.

12 Go over the central spaces with white and color in the nose, tongue and round the eyes.

TIP

☞ **Staples** are strong and are useful when attaching different parts together, such as the elastic on the cat mask.

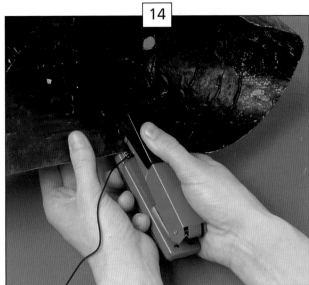

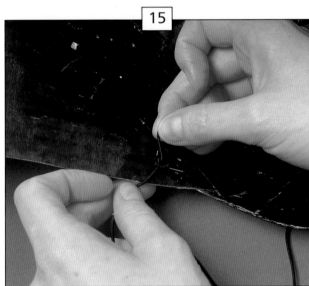

13 Paint over the eye pupils with black ink and cover the ears and sides of the mask and whiskers.

14 Fix staples at the base of ears.

15 Tie the hat elastic to these.

TIP

☞ **Glass-paper** is for rubbing down unsightly edges and creases in papier-mâché.

Maracas

Use these to beat a rhythm from the land where the orange trees grow.
Make the colors hot too!

YOU WILL NEED

- An orange
- Petroleum jelly
- Newsprint
- Wallpaper (or cellulose) paste
- Mat knife
- Lentils (1 teaspoon)
- Corrugated card, 8" x 6" (with ribbing 8" long)
- Black construction paper, 6" x 4" and a circle to fit handle end – approx. ¾" diameter
- Tissue paper scraps in orange, red and black
- PVA glue
- Brown gummed paper tape
- Wire cooling rack

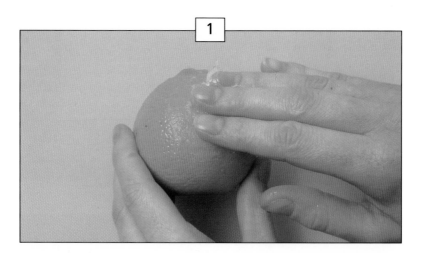

1 Grease the orange lightly with petroleum jelly.

2 Paste onto the orange 8 layers of small strips of newsprint. Use different colored strips to help to tell when each layer is finished.

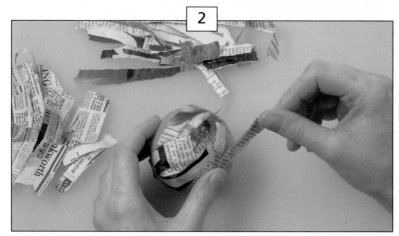

3 **When it has dried out completely (after 2 days in a warm place on the rack) cut around the casting, in a straight line, with a mat knife until almost to the end. Remove the orange and throw it away.**

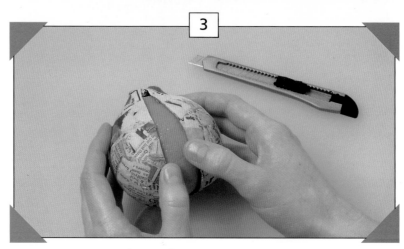

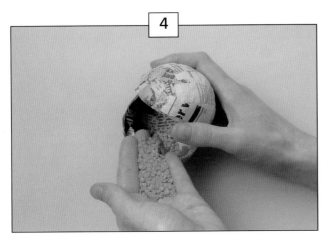

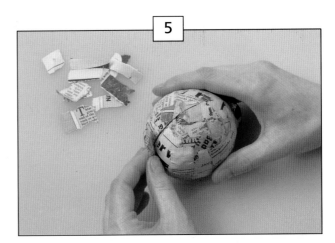

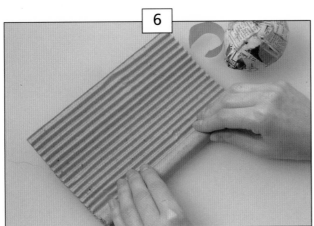

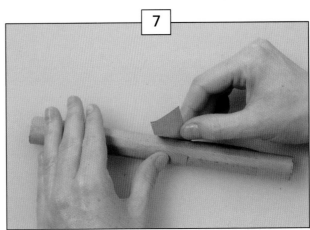

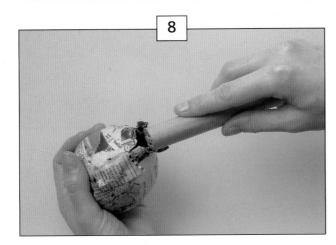

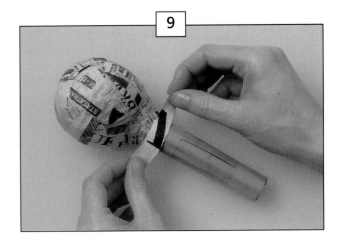

4 Add some lentils to one half and close up the casting.

5 Paste small pieces of newsprint all around the join.

6 Roll up the corrugated card into an 8" long rod.

7 Seal it round with brown gummed paper tape.

8 Gently push one end inside the end of the orange casting.

9 Join up the handle to the casting with more layers of pasted newsprint. Leave to dry for 30 minutes in a warm place.

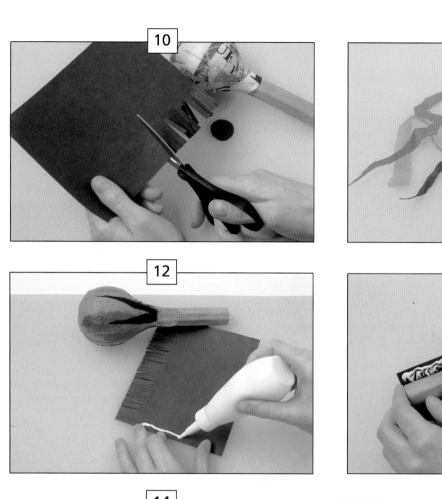

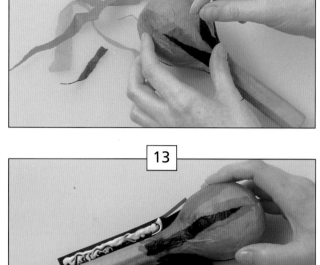

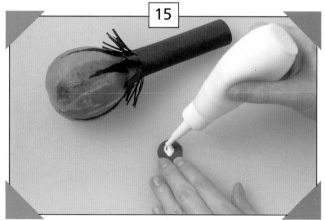

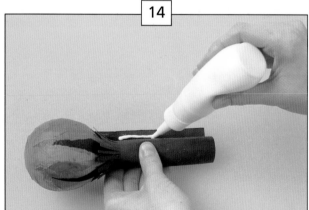

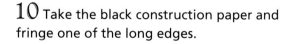

10 Take the black construction paper and fringe one of the long edges.

11 Tear up strips of orange, red and black tissue paper and then paste them evenly around the maraca head and smooth over.

12 Take the piece of black paper again and put glue along one short side.

13 Stick this along the handle with the fringe around the head and continue rolling it up.

14 Then seal the opposite end with more glue.

15 **Cut a circle of black to fit end of handle.**

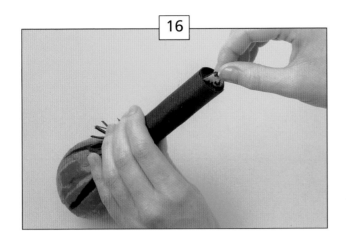

16 Stick this just inside the end of the handle.

17 Cover with dilute PVA to varnish and protect.

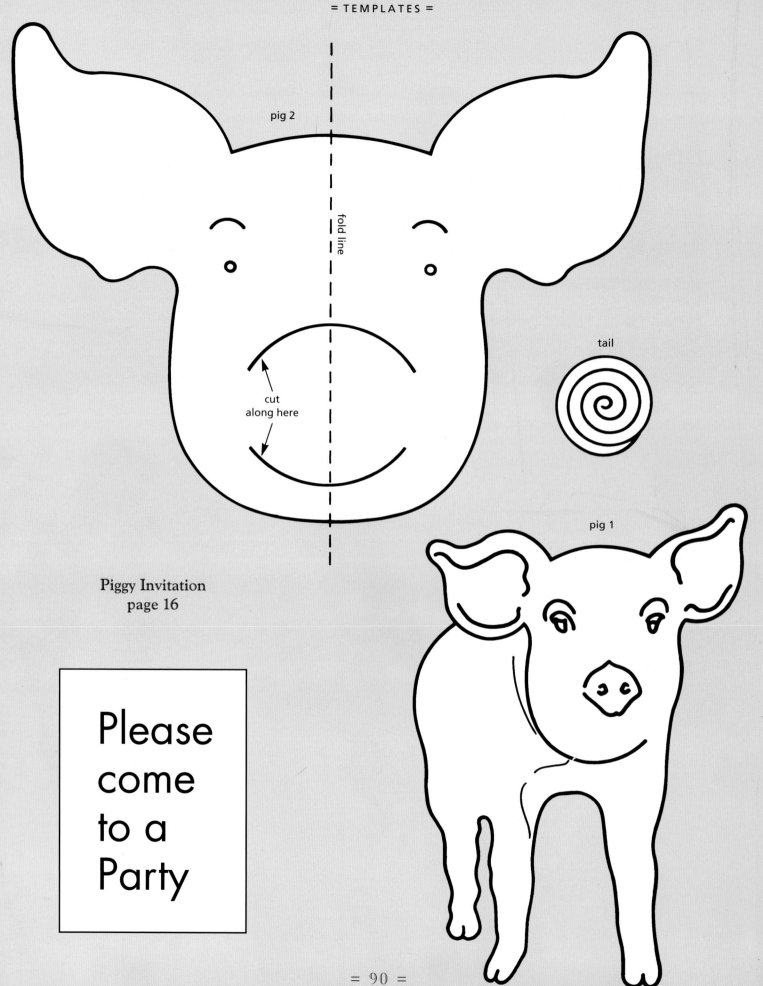

pig 2

fold line

tail

cut
along here

Piggy Invitation
page 16

pig 1

Please
come
to a
Party

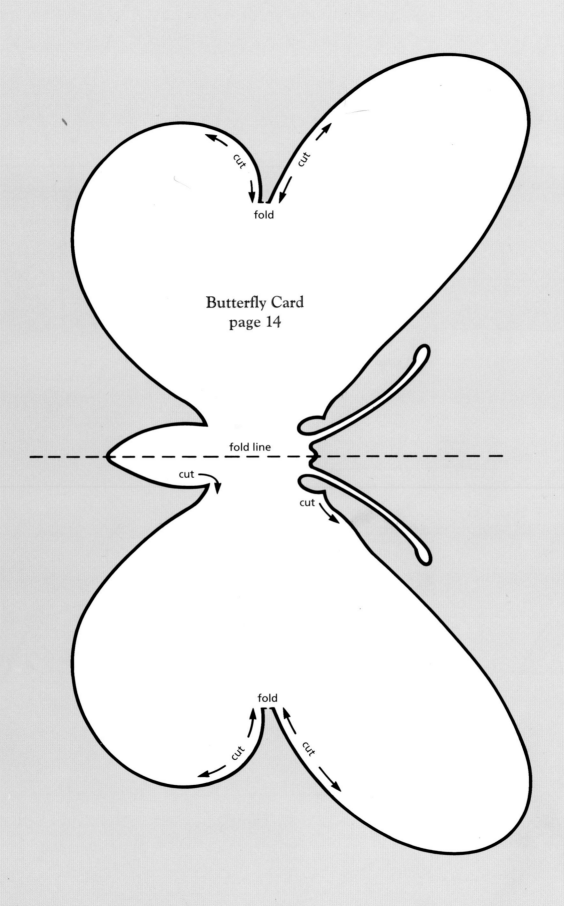

Butterfly Card
page 14

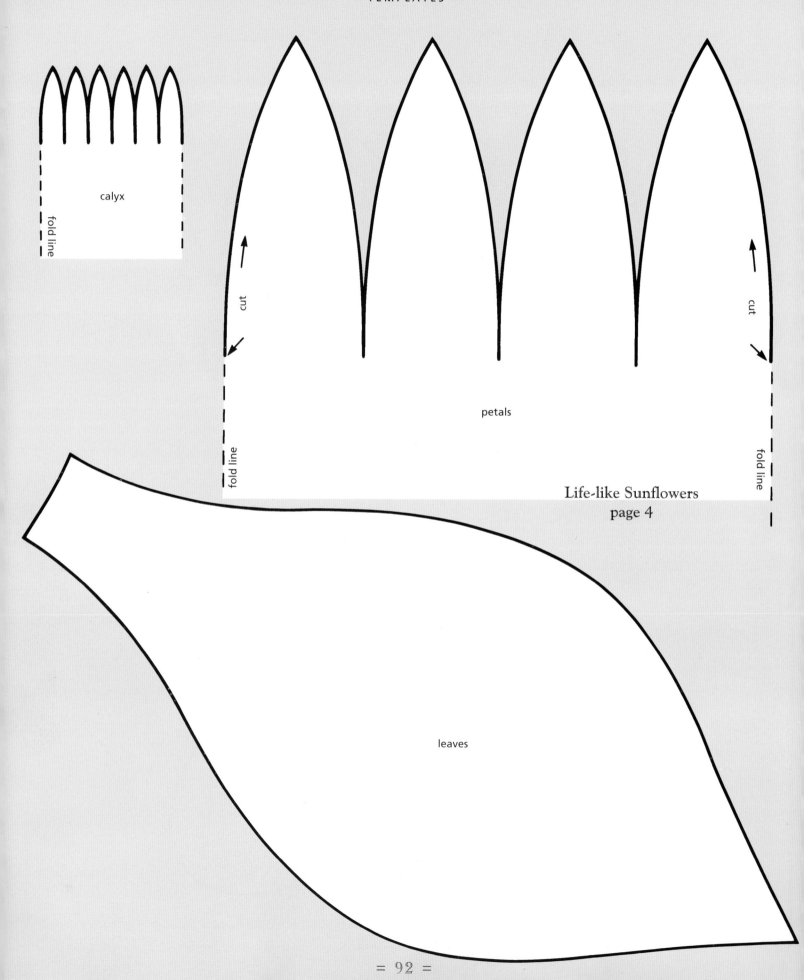

calyx

fold line

cut

cut

fold line

petals

fold line

Life-like Sunflowers
page 4

leaves

Outside Candle Lantern page 50

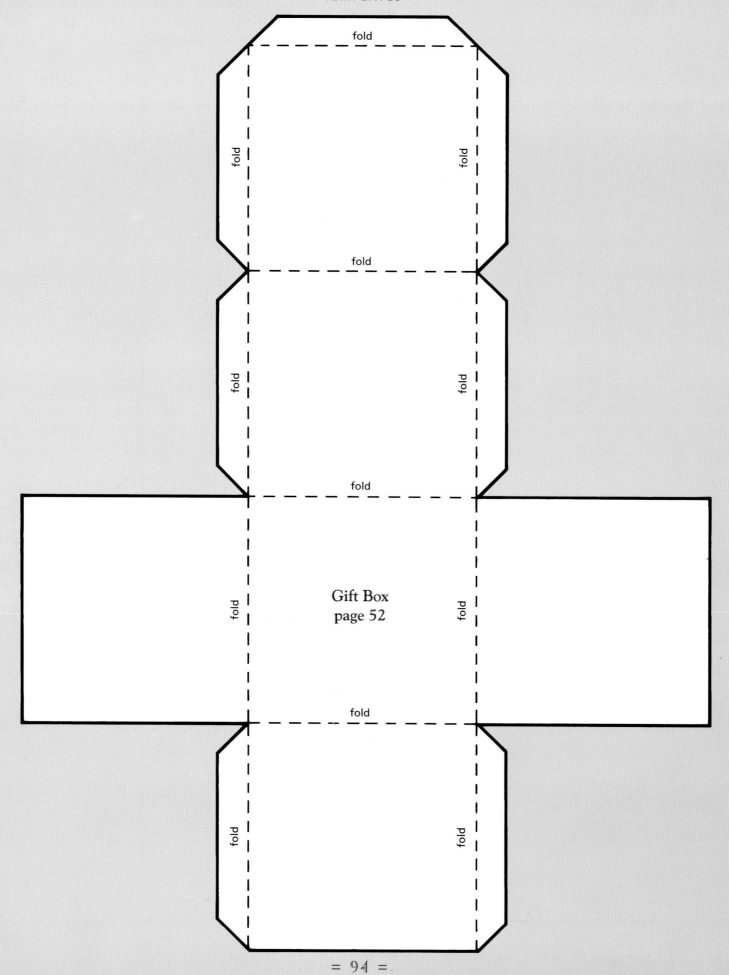

fold

fold

fold

fold

fold

fold

fold

fold

fold

Gift Box
page 52

fold

fold

fold

fold

fold

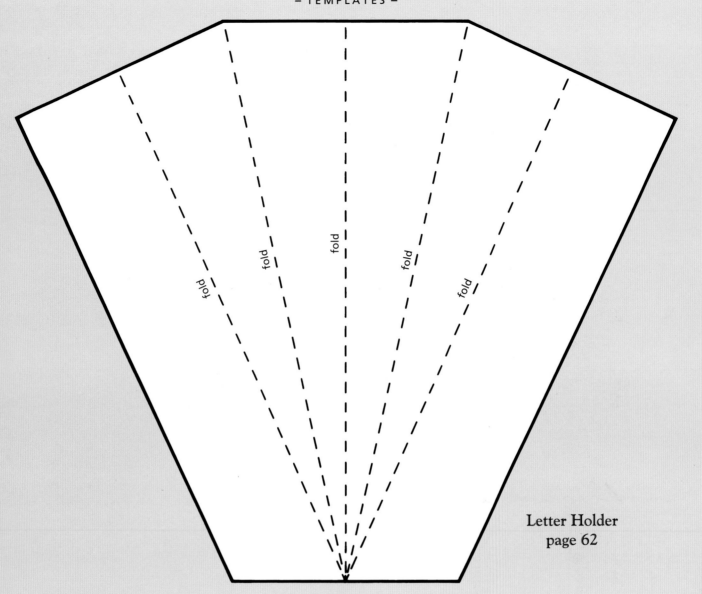

Letter Holder
page 62

3' long

Clown Puppet
page 75

ruff

sew

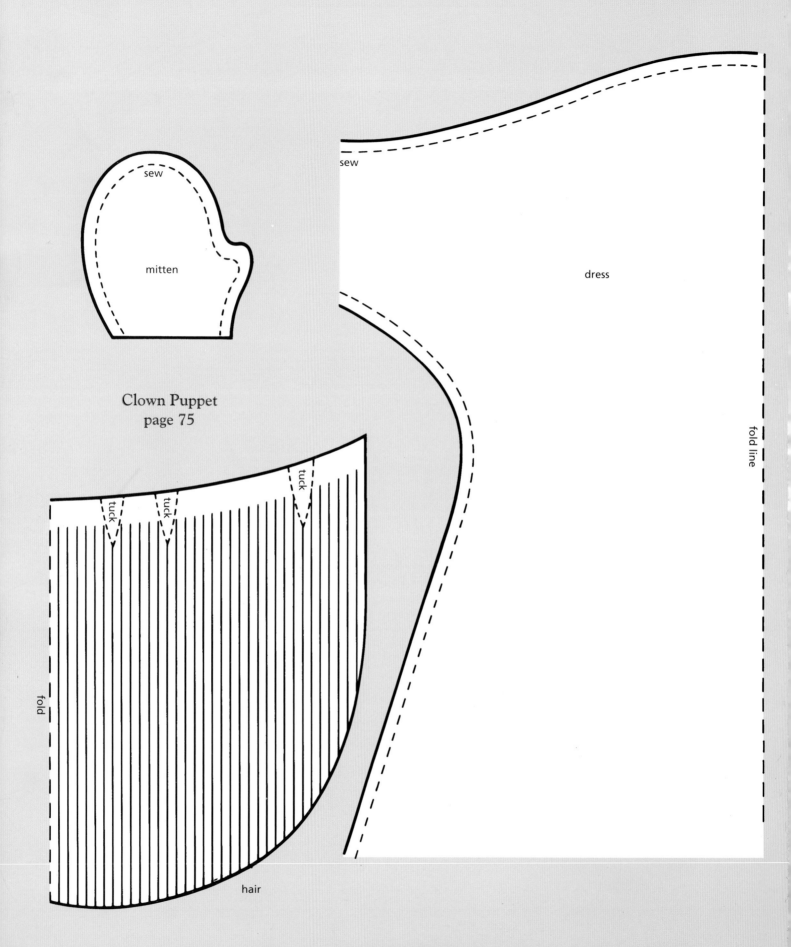

sew

sew

mitten

dress

Clown Puppet
page 75

fold line

tuck

tuck

tuck

fold

hair